Reality is

The Art of Impror

Anthony Jacquin

This work is owned and published by Anthony Jacquin of UKHTC Ltd..

UKHTC Ltd. was set up in 1999 and is an internationally recognized training centre in the art of hypnosis and hypnotherapy. UKHTC specialise in the provision of training products and courses.

Reality is Plastic: The Art of Impromptu Hypnosis

First published 2007
Reprinted with revisions 2008
© Anthony Jacquin 2007, 2008

Photography by Red Square Photography Studio and Vivid Creative Ideas.
Graphic design by Overthrow Productions Ltd. www.overthrowproductions.com

Anthony Jacquin
Room 6-8 St. James St.
Derby,
Derbyshire DE1 1RF
United Kingdom
Email: enquiries@anthonyjacquin.com
Web: www.anthonyjacquin.com

ISBN: 978-0-9559084-0-8

Reality is Plastic!

The Art of Impromptu Hypnosis

Anthony Jacquin

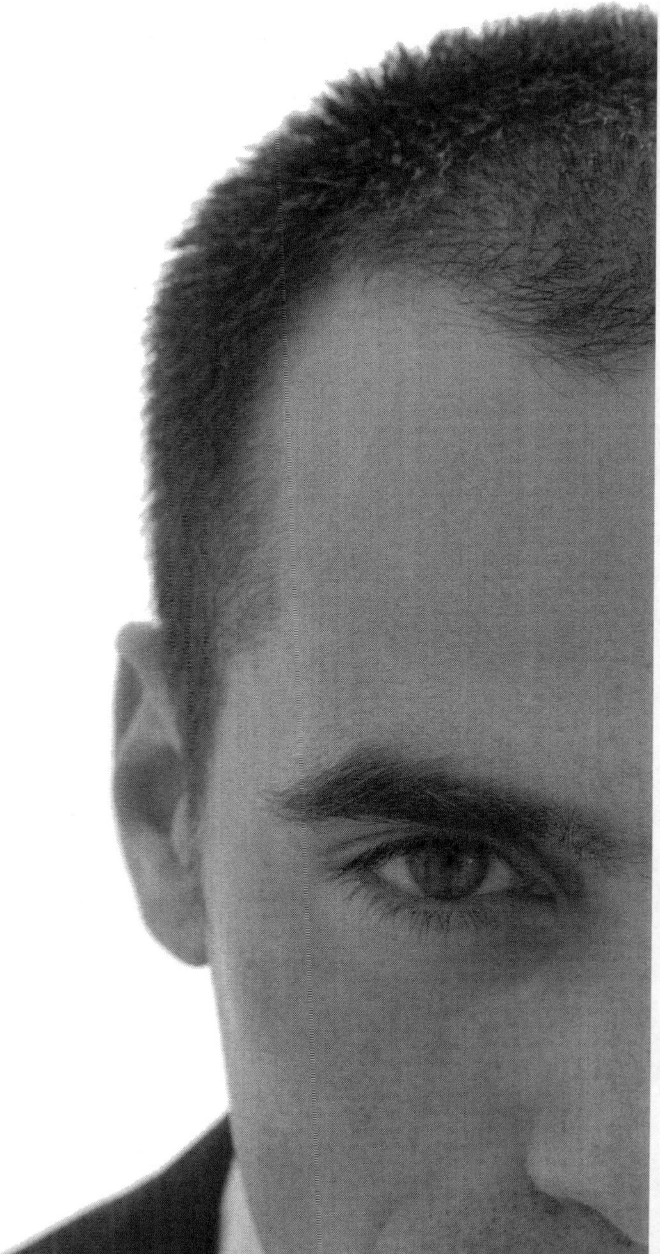

About Reality is Plastic: The Art of Impromptu Hypnosis

This book is a resource for those professing to be or wishing to become hypnotists. It is not a substitute for hands on training from a professional hypnotist who is accomplished at delivering training. However if you follow the guidelines in this book and have the right attitude, aptitude, as well as enough front, talent and confidence you will hypnotize people.

With this ability comes responsibility. Hypnosis can be used for fun, to create laughter and produce wonderful therapeutic changes in people. It can just as easily result in confusion, fear and unhelpful changes. If you know what you are doing then the chances of causing even temporary distress or upset are extremely small. With this in mind this book closes with information about how to use hypnosis in a way that ensures the wellbeing of all concerned is taken care of. Please read this chapter and use your common sense with regard to health and safety and decent morals and ethics with regard to the direction you apply hypnosis.

Throughout this book and my other training products and courses I offer suggestions for words, phrases and in some cases complete scripts that will be useful to you. However my emphasis when training people is that to be a good hypnotist you must first become The Hypnotist and think of yourself as The Hypnotist. Your attitude, persona and confidence carry more weight than any script or linguistic trick. Where I have offered suggestions for what to say please understand that these are the words I use - they work for me. I have belief in them. In some cases they may seem very brief but I can assure you nothing has been left out. Nothing superfluous added. When hypnotizing I use these words and techniques over and over without a huge amount of variation, just some personalisation depending on whom I am addressing. In that sense they have become my patter or script. Do not feel you must repeat them verbatim - although that is not a bad place to start if you are a complete beginner. Use them as a starting point. The words you use to do your work as The Hypnotist must sound right to you. They must be easily understood and resonate with those you address. You are going to use them to focus the attention of your subject and suggest ideas to them.

Take these ideas and branch off from them. Develop your own style of patter and you will be more effective. Scripts are not spells and should not be read. It is not the words that do the hypnotising, you do. Even if you use the words I use exactly as they are given, ensure that you take ownership of them; rehearse over and over and over until they become part of you.

A number of conventions have been used to make any scripted portions of the book easier to understand.

- Throughout we will refer to the Hypnotist as 'The Hypnotist'.
- Throughout we will refer to the person being hypnotized as 'the subject'.
- General text and any descriptive instructions are written in this plain text. These instructions should NOT be spoken to the subject.
- Any words or instructions that are spoken to the subject are in **bold**.

In hypnosis you are primarily going to use words to influence your subject. So you had better know what you are saying. Aim to become a master of communication. Reflect upon the words you use and their meanings and associations. You should pay attention to how you deliver suggestions and how best to instruct your subject. Learn to use your vocal tone and tempo to communicate your intention clearly and understand when to use silence and emphasis. All of this will help you improve your communication skills generally and help you become an excellent hypnotist. You will swiftly begin to develop your own favoured suggestions and style.

There is nothing wrong with imitating. It is one way of learning. So watch shows and clips of the best hypnotists at work. Read around the subject too. The best hypnotists appear totally confident, expecting nothing less than complete success. They appear knowledgeable and totally certain about what they are doing. Ultimately be yourself – just more so.

1.0 What is Impromptu Hypnosis?

This book is about hypnosis and how to use it effectively. It will teach you what hypnosis is and how to hypnotize both individuals and groups of people any time and anywhere you choose.

This is not a book on stage hypnosis nor is it a book on hypnotherapy or self hypnosis or mentalism. It is not about accelerated learning, covert speed seduction or persuasive sales. It is not about old original hypnosis or new fandangled hypnosis. Many things can be achieved with hypnosis but they are the results of hypnosis – not hypnosis itself. The hypnosis you will learn in this book can be applied in all of the situations above and any other area of your life.

No prior experience of hypnosis is required to understand and apply the knowledge in this book. The techniques are deceptively simple yet incredibly powerful. They are entirely practical and have been road tested over many years with thousands of people in my therapy and entertainment work. When you have mastered them you may well find they are all you need. That said there is always more to learn. So make hypnosis your art form. Be prepared to put in the time and effort required to master your craft.

To bring this approach to hypnotising into a practical context this book is focussed on how to provide impromptu demonstrations of hypnosis that can be applied in any setting. This could be for the purposes of fun, entertainment and laughter. It could be rapid relief from physical and mental pains or for the purposes of hypnotic engineering*. How you apply it is up to you.

---

*Hypnotic engineering is a term coined by a fellow hypnotist, security expert and friend Kev Sheldrake. It stems from 'social engineering' the practice in the hacking world of getting required physical access to places or information (such as passwords) out of people 'wetware' rather than by using software or hardware. The term is used here in a wider social context and applies to acquiring material goods and services as well as information – engineering people to do what you want them to do.

When you introduce yourself as a Hypnotist, or if people learn that you can hypnotize, very often they will ask if you can hypnotize them. When you say 'yes' they will often ask if you can do it right then. This book is an instructional on how best to make the most of these opportunities. It will also show you how to create a context for hypnosis so you can introduce it to any situation you wish.

Far too many people, who claim to be able to hypnotize well, especially hypnotherapists, do not feel confident to give an impromptu demonstration of hypnosis and will make an excuse regarding why they would rather not hypnotize in a party or other social setting. This has much to do with many training courses for hypnotherapy emphasising the use of long progressive inductions often with a large emphasis on relaxation and little or no cultivation of hypnotic phenomena. It also has something to do with a little bit of fear – principally the fear of failing and looking foolish.

The progressive approach works fine when done well, however it is not the most appropriate induction for impromptu hypnosis or the most effective. If turning down an opportunity to hypnotize is a professional call based on not wishing to appear to take hypnosis anything less than seriously then fair enough. However if it is based on a lack of ideas about how to proceed then this book will address that gap in knowledge.

I got into hypnosis by using it for therapeutic purposes and became a hypnotherapist before I started using it for entertainment. I spend much of my working day as a hypnotherapist using hypnosis to help people change the way they think, feel and respond to things in their life. I specialise in the kind of hypnotherapy that is sometimes described as brief or rapid or solution focussed. This approach to change does not involve counselling or analysis, instead it focuses on changing the mental patterns or programmes a person uses in their daily life. I hugely enjoy this work.

I also love having fun with hypnosis to entertain people. I do traditional stage hypnosis but also perform close up in the same way a strolling magician might entertain at a party or function. My close up performance might be described as a cross between Hypnotism and Mentalism, and creates the impression I can force people to act or respond in certain ways, read their behaviour and predict their actions. I have also done work with various TV companies that required me to use hypnosis with an unsuspecting public on the street and in a variety of public places including shops, restaurants, clubs and places of work.

I use the approach outlined in this book in all of these settings. It fits whether I am in the therapy room showing someone how to overcome a phobia, in a pub 'sticking' someone's feet to the floor or on stage giving a performance. Hypnosis is hypnosis whether it takes place in a therapy room, party or sports field. Understanding that your subject does not have to be sitting in a comfy chair in a therapy room listening to whale music to be hypnotized goes a short way to helping you be good at impromptu hypnosis.

One of the seemingly unanswerable questions in philosophy is 'Do we all see red the same way?'

Fortunately we do not need to answer that question to be able to hypnotize. However it is useful to proceed with the assumption that our personal perception of reality is just a malleable point of view. All that exists are pseudo events and objects to which we adjust with a false consciousness adapted to see these things as true and real. Hypnosis literally changes our perception of reality, it gives us another false consciousness that we adapt to as being as true and real as the last – in this sense reality is plastic.

Some of my experimental research and performance work has required me to test some common ideas about how best to induce hypnosis and also what you can do with people when they have been hypnotized. Some of that work, although highly questionable from an ethical perspective, offered a great opportunity to test some of the perceived limits of hypnosis. Even as an experienced practitioner of hypnosis and hypnotherapy, I was still surprised to find just how far this relatively well-understood discipline could really be pushed when taken out of the confines of the therapy room or stage performance.

- Is it possible to walk into a shop/office/market, talk to a member of staff for a few minutes and leave with anything you choose without paying?
- Is it possible to pay people with pieces of rubbish instead of cash/card?
- Can you make people treat you like a superstar?
- Can you make people corpse with laughter on command?
- Is it possible to become 'invisible'?

The answer to all of these questions and many more just like it is yes. The directions this can be taken are endless.

The techniques in this book are simple, direct and can be learnt. They can be applied effectively in a real world setting, well out of the comfort zone of the hypnotherapy room and without the luxury of a stage full of expectant hypnotic subjects. They can be used anywhere the subject can hear you. They are entirely impromptu.

2.0 Hypnosis: No introduction necessary

Whether someone believes in hypnosis or not, whether they have experienced it or not, they are still likely to have a strong personal concept of what hypnosis is and how it typically proceeds. This may be based on something they have read, seen in movies or on T.V shows. They may have first hand experience as a subject or spectator or just be relying on hearsay and urban myth. Even most children by the age of 7 or 8 have a concept of hypnosis.

So before we begin it might be useful to ask yourself a few questions and note what you come up with.

Firstly, what do you think hypnosis is? What images spring to mind when you think of hypnosis, hypnotists and the hypnotized? Which words or phrases would a hypnotist most commonly use? What does it feel like to be hypnotized? How do people act when hypnotized? Do you think you can be hypnotized? Can hypnotists make you do things against your will?

When you have learnt more about hypnosis and accept yourself as The Hypnotist it is likely that your ideas about what hypnosis is and how it can be used will be quite different from the view of the general public. It is wise not to forget what most people believe it to be. Using their mental models of hypnosis is fine - even if they are not that accurate – just as long as their model does not leave them afraid of hypnosis for some reason. If it does then it is useful to remove their fears prior to hypnotising them and this is simple enough to do.

I have asked hundreds of students of hypnosis, thousands of therapy clients and many hypnotists the question, 'What do you think hypnosis is?'

The answers vary quite dramatically, even amongst hypnotists. However several common themes run throughout the public perception of this art.

Sleep, a relaxed state, swinging watches, stage hypnosis, getting in touch with the subconscious, telling someone what to do, a comfy chair, a slow sleepy or gravely voice, a snap of the fingers and more recently Little Britain and the phrase 'you're under'* are common answers when the general public try to give you a sense of what they think hypnosis is all about.

Images of people slumped in a chair with their eyes closed under the mesmerizing gaze and command of the hypnotist might come to mind. A row of empty chairs, 'sleeping' subjects, people doing ridiculous things or experiencing amnesia are also relatively common ideas.

Even in our modern rather sceptical society popular belief often still ascribes some significance to the devices and rituals of hypnosis such as making passes with the hands, spinning hypnotic watches, spirals, the hypnotic stare and the authoritarian command. A few years ago my wife gave me a pocket watch on a chain as a present. The first time I got it out to show some friends in a pub they scattered – as if looking at it would immediately put them under.

There are dozens of definitions of hypnosis – some more accurate than others and most quite unsatisfactory. Whatever definition is in vogue does not seem to affect a great deal of change in the actual practical application of hypnosis or the phenomena elicited.

Definitions often describe hypnosis as a 'state' of some kind. Just what kind of state however is up for debate. A 'state like sleep', 'a unique or special state', 'a trance state', 'any altered state' and of course 'a relaxed state'. These definitions all have some value but upon examination can all be found to be equally unsatisfactory.

Little Britain is a British comedy show written and starring Matt Lucas and David Williams. It featured a character called Kenny Craig a cliché caricature; he is an obnoxious and charmless hypnotist who uses his powers to get his own way.

Given that we are always in a state of some kind and many studies have found little significant difference between someone in hypnosis and someone in a normal state, critics of these definitions suggest that hypnosis cannot be defined in terms of state. Some go as far to say that because hypnosis cannot be proved to be a unique state hypnosis does not exist. All of that said, with recent advances in brain scanning equipment more evidence is coming forward that there are significant changes in brain function when hypnotized.

Another way to define hypnosis is as a process or an art. Certainly it is possible to be an excellent hypnotist without knowledge of psychology or brain function or state theory. Talent, flair and the pure force of personality will take you far as a hypnotist. So will accepting that hypnosis is really just the artful application of suggestion to someone who is in a focussed state.

Hippolyte Bernheim (1840-1919) the Father of 20th century Hypnosis, famously said,

'It is suggestion that rules hypnotism'
Hippolyte Bernheim (1).

He believed hypnosis was inherently a suggestion based process. It is a useful assumption although difficult to get to grips with scientifically.

Although trance has certainly been used for the purposes of healing and as an aid to creativity for thousands of years we really trace the trance we call hypnosis back to the work of an Austrian physician, Franz Anton Mesmer (1734-1815). Mesmer came up with a theory and a way of treating people that helped many to health. His ideas were based almost entirely on untested hypothesis and faulty science, but they led to more accurate ideas about hypnosis in the nineteenth century.

Mesmer believed that among all the fields known to science at that time there was another field, which might be called an animate field or fluid or life force. He defined good health as the free flow of this field or fluid through thousands of channels in our bodies. Illness resulted from obstructions to the free flow of this fluid. Overcoming these obstacles and restoring flow restored health. When nature failed to do this spontaneously, contact with a conductor of 'animal magnetism' was a necessary and sufficient remedy. Mesmer in other words believed that he was a conductor of animal magnetism and that this could influence the flow of the fluid like life force. Mesmer aimed to aid Natures effort to heal. He treated patients both individually and in groups. With individuals he would sit in front of his patient with his knees touching the patient's knees, pressing the patient's thumbs in his hands, looking fixedly into the patient's eyes. Mesmer made "passes", moving his hands from patient's shoulders down along their arms. Prior to him it was common practice to do this with magnets. Many patients felt peculiar sensations or had convulsions that were regarded as crises that were supposed to bring about the cure (2).

In the nineteenth century the idea that there was some invisible fluid or influence travelling from the hypnotist to the subject crumbled and eventually hypnosis became viewed by many as something that the subject is responsible for, or more accurately capable of, given the right instruction. This eventually led some to conclude that all hypnosis is self hypnosis. More recently hypnosis has become viewed by many as a peculiarity of the social relationship between the hypnotist and the subject – the hypnotist and the subject 'playing' their parts as they believe they should. In other words it is social compliance or role play.

The debate has gone on for decades and will probably continue to do so. For our purposes we will look at the definitions of arguably the most influential hypnotists that walked the planet, James Braid, Milton Erickson and Dave Elman.

James Braid (1795 – 1860) caused a paradigm shift from the mesmerists of the 18th and early 19th century. Braid was a Doctor and after observing a demonstration of mesmerism believed he had figured out why people went into this peculiar state and it had nothing to do with an invisible magnetic fluid. He suggested a physiological basis for hypnosis. It is generally agreed that his initial insightful but inaccurate view was that the mesmerised state (hypnosis) was caused by the tiring of an optic nerve as it became fixated – hence the association with focussing on spinning watches or in his case a silver cigarette case. It seems he missed the fact that his verbal suggestions to his subjects that their eyes would feel tired were also having an effect. Later in his writings he seems to shift emphasis, although does not abandon eye fixation altogether, noting that it is not just the gaze that becomes fixated but the minds eye as well. In other words when hypnotized the mind becomes locked around a single idea.

'The real origin and essence of the hypnotic condition is the induction of a habit of abstraction or mental concentration, in which, as in reverie or spontaneous abstraction, the powers of the mind are so much engrossed with a single idea or train of thought, as, for the nonce, to render the individual unconscious of, or indifferently conscious to, all other ideas, impressions, or trains of thought.'
James Braid (3).

Note that Braid says hypnosis renders the individual unconscious or indifferently conscious to all other ideas. This is important. When hypnotized you can still have an experience you can reflect on as you are having it and as far as you are concerned a fully conscious experience. For example if you are hypnotized to believe you cannot remove your hand from your face because it has been glued there, you are still able to reflect on the fact that it is stuck and even wonder why it is stuck. However the only reality you have is that it is stuck nonetheless. If you are hypnotized to believe that beer bottle tops are pound coins then even when pointed out that they are bottle tops you will know without doubt or question that they are not bottle tops they are coins and will accept them as such. You are indifferent to ideas other than the one your mind has locked onto as reality.

The hypnotist directs the subject's perception of reality by locking the mind around ideas.

From the time of Braid right up into the twentieth century hypnosis was typically induced using a direct and authoritarian approach.

In the 20th Century Milton Erickson (1901 – 1980) caused a seismic shift in the way to induce hypnosis, developing a permissive and indirect approach that is very popular with 21st Century Hypnotherapists. By the end of his career he appeared to simply be having conversations with his patients who would go into trance without any mention of the word hypnosis. Of course Erickson knew exactly what he was saying and what he was doing and why it caused hypnosis. His insights with regard to personal change have revolutionised modern therapy. I encourage you to read his work and you will discover many incredible ways you can use hypnosis. He experimented with hypnosis pretty much every day from 1920 to 1980. He covered a lot of ground. Because his permissive approach to hypnosis is so popular, it is often overlooked that Erickson was a master of rapid direct impromptu hypnosis too and would use it just as readily as the more cultivated covert or indirect approach. It is said he used the handshake induction so often that by the end of his career no one actually wanted to shake his hand. Many of his statements have been quoted as his definition of hypnosis – all are worth reading. What follows is just one of them.

'A state of special awareness characterized by receptiveness to ideas.'
Milton Erickson (4).

Two things are worth noting from this succinct definition. He emphasises that the mind becomes receptive to the ideas the hypnotist presents. This can be interpreted as a person becoming more suggestible or more open to the ideas being presented to them when they are hypnotized. The emphasis Erickson places on 'awareness' rather than on being unconscious, inattentive or unaware is also interesting. It is in line with his thinking that hypnosis allows you to deal with the bigger beast in all of us, the subconscious mind or what he called the unconscious mind. When hypnotized, the unconscious seems to assume more responsibility or come to the fore. The unconscious regulates all of your bodily processes, stores and manages your memories, every learning from every experience as well as the mental patterns and templates that allow us to function. This part of the mind is intuitive. It can call up your potential's and instantly change the way you think, feel and respond. By contrast the conscious mind is limited. It is logical and linear in its approach to problem solving. It is the here and now.

Erickson was not interested in talking to the conscious mind. Neither should you be when you are in the process of hypnotising. Aim to communicate directly with the unconscious.

Finally, consider one of the most well known and quoted definitions from a modern innovator and perhaps the most influential hypnotist of all time, Dave Elman (1900 – 1967).

'Hypnosis is a state of mind in which the critical faculty of the human is bypassed, and selective thinking established.'
Dave Elman (5).

Elman refers to a state where '…the critical faculty of the human is bypassed…'.

So what is the critical faculty? It does not seem to correlate to any physical part of the brain or neurological process. It is more conceptual – think of it as being a filter between the conscious and unconscious minds. It can be thought of as the sense of judgement. It has certain characteristics. It is rational, logical, it is limited and it is typified by inductive thinking – proceeding from certain facts to a logical conclusion.

The critical faculty is the bit of you that thinks it knows what reality is. It thinks it knows hot from cold. It thinks it knows that a mop is not the person you are in love with. It thinks it will hurt if you stick a needle through your arm. It thinks that you could lift your feet up if you wished to. It believes you do know your own name.

Bypassing the critical faculty does not establish hypnosis, but it does represent, as Elman put it, the 'entering wedge.'

When the critical faculty is bypassed, your sense of judgement, inductive reasoning and logical faculties become suspended or inattentive. How inattentive and for how long they remain suspended is reliant on the attitude of the subject and the ability of the hypnotist. When attitude and ability are both conducive to hypnosis the unconscious mind of your subject becomes dominant and with further direction from the hypnotist selective thinking can be established swiftly. According to Elman, selective thinking is whatever you believe wholeheartedly.

By unconscious mind I mean everything else other than the conscious critical mind – all of your memories, every learning, resource, pattern and template. By selective thinking I mean a style of thinking where inductive reasoning is suspended and the mind becomes locked around an idea. When this occurs The Hypnotists suggestions will be listened to by the unconscious uncritically. They will be acted upon uncritically.

That does not mean the unconscious cannot refuse to go in your direction, it can. It does not mean the critical faculty will continue to remain bypassed; it can pop back into play. However as The Hypnotist understand and be clear that to all intents and purposes hypnotising someone results in their unquestioning acceptance of the ideas, suggestions and directions delivered by The Hypnotist.

The critical faculty can be bypassed in a variety of ways quite naturally without hypnosis. Experiencing confusion, shock, high emotion, information overload, being drunk or high on drugs, laughter, play and performance are all common instances where are sense of judgement and logic can be temporarily suspended. It is the rabbit in the headlights moment. Whatever follows is generally driven by our unconscious, instinctive, automatic mind. The Hypnotist can create such moments artificially and utilise the result to establish selective thinking. The techniques that follow in section three will show you how to do that.

It is useful to note that in none of these definitions is there any mention of sleep or relaxation. That is because hypnosis is not sleep and does not require even a smidgen of relaxation. What is emphasised is that when hypnotized the subject's attention narrows and becomes fixed around selected ideas or a single idea. Wider environmental stimuli are ignored.

Recently a fresh theory of hypnosis and the mind entranced has emerged from the Human Givens pioneers Jo Griffin and Ivan Tyrell (6). They suggest that hypnosis is the result of accessing the REM state. In the REM state we access the imagination, what they refer to as 'the reality generator', that is responsible for our dreams. One of the functions of dreaming is to discharge unresolved emotional arousal. In another words it allows us to complete emotional ruminations of the day through the metaphoric imagery and connections of our dream. Its other key function is to update our instinctive templates or behavioural and emotional responses. In other words the learning state is also an REM state. Whenever we act without conscious effort we are reliant on pattern matching, going back to an earlier learned response or behaviour that was set in the REM state. So when we act instinctively we are, in effect, acting on a post hypnotic suggestion. In the same way when a hypnotized subject acts on a post hypnotic suggestion given by the hypnotist they will do so with the same effectiveness, immediacy and instinct they do other unconscious behaviours.

So when we put someone into hypnosis we are simply activating the same processes that the brain activates during dream sleep, including the reality generator - this is what makes it so effective.

For your purposes as The Hypnotist it is useful to keep these definitions in mind. Revisit them in light of your experience. Read the work of those who coined them. However there really is no need to get hung up on exactly what hypnosis is or why it occurs. There is no point being concerned over whether the 'critical faculty' is something we can pin point physically or not. Even less point trying to prove that hypnosis is real.

The mind exists as a model. Hypnosis exists as a phenomenon. We must use a conceptual model to describe how it works. Hypnosis may not have the reality of a house brick but that is of no consequence to you. The fact is you can hold any of the major views about hypnosis and still be a good hypnotist.

For practical purposes as The Hypnotist think of it this way.

'Hypnosis is the art of presenting ideas directly to the receptive unconscious mind.'
Anthony Jacquin

So understand, as The Hypnotist you are presenting ideas and giving directions. You are doing this to your subject's unconscious mind and it is receptive to the directions and ideas you are presenting. Believe, want and expect that it will interpret them and act on them with a genuine unconscious response.

2.1 Being The Hypnotist

To be a great hypnotist it is of key importance that you become The Hypnotist. Not a hypnotist. Not someone who knows a bit about hypnosis but The Hypnotist. You must express absolute confidence, congruence and expertise in your skills, knowledge and abilities. In the beginning this takes a certain amount of front. Pretend and master it. Believe you are the best, believe you are a natural and behave like you are.

Believe your subject is a wonderful hypnotic subject. Want and expect them to go into hypnosis and do what you tell them. It is often said that close friends and family are your worst subjects because they cannot accept you as the hypnotist.

It is sometimes harder for them to enter into that reality than people who do not know you so well. But do not fret; just have a go at hypnotising everyone and anyone who will put up with you, including close friends and family. It may be that a family member or friend is a superb subject and you will have your own hypno monkey for life.

2.2 Setting things up

When you have decided to hypnotize someone or someone asks if you would there are five things it is useful to do.

- Remove fear
- Eliminate misconceptions
- Increase expectancy
- Fire up the imagination
- Take control

When a stage hypnotist works, if they are doing their job properly they will have already fired up their audience imagination and created a great deal of expectation that something is going to happen with the promotion of their show. Amongst their opening patter they typically spend a few minutes going over the reasons why everyone can rest assured they are safe, in the hands of an expert and have reason to feel excited and have fun. The audience should certainly know who is in control.

In a therapy room this is all helped by the advertising, hypnotherapy certificate and the ramble about how the subject remains in control of themselves and aware of everything.

In impromptu hypnosis setting things up needs to be accomplished more swiftly - often in a few sentences. Often in a few seconds.

The easiest approach is to just ignore all of the above and take control. This means rapidly hypnotize the subject in seconds or less, before they have a chance to be afraid. Using a rapid induction such as the Instant Induction, Jacquin Power Induction or Handshake Induction detailed in Section Four will do that. However if you are not going to do that, a few simple words will help things along.

There is no point getting into a 30 minute explanation of what hypnosis is all about. A few choice words will do it. This is in effect your elevator pitch. Your elevator pitch is what you would say to Bill Gates or Richard Branson in a short ride in a lift. In brief clear terms what you would say to them if you had just a few seconds to sell your idea (7).

With hypnosis you are selling the ideas that you can hypnotize, that your subject can be hypnotized and that there is no need to be concerned as you will look after them. So tell them you are a hypnotist. They will immediately wonder if they could be hypnotized or if you are already hypnotizing them.

Fear of hypnosis takes a few forms. Firstly your subject may fear the unknown. So let them know hypnosis is simply a wonderful state of mind. Let them know it is not sleep and that they will be able to hear you. They may fear that they will immediately reveal some secret information and embarrass or ruin themselves. Assure them they will not. They may fear they will get stuck in a trance or never be the same. Assure them that they cannot get stuck in a trance. Let them know it will be an enjoyable experience. Let them know they will find it interesting and will learn something about themselves. They may fear you – this is not ideal unless they fear you can hypnotize them in a flash.

Taking control does not mean being bossy and pushy but it does require you to become the dominant party. This can be achieved by asking your subject to do something.

Can you just move your chair to one side slightly. Now can you place your feet on the floor, your hands comfortably in your lap and look at me.

If they are standing up, then adjust their position and ask them to put their feet together.

It begins to demonstrate who is in control and you get a chance to see how good the subject is at taking directions. Some of the inductions and Set Pieces in this book are best carried out with the subject starting in a particular physical position and mental state so use this bit of psychological bullying to tidy them up at the same time.

Everything you ask them to do, however small the instruction or request may seem, must be done with one purpose in mind – to get them doing what you want them to. Remember your subject probably does not know how hypnosis proceeds. So give them the comfort of knowing who is in control.

As soon as you have said to someone you are a hypnotist then their expectation that they might get hypnotized and their imagination about what might happen have already begun to fire up. You should leverage this your advantage.

Get rid of any of your own fears about whether they will go into hypnosis or not or whether you will look like a fool if they do not. Eliminate your own misconceptions about what kind of subject they might or might not be. Help these processes along by being genuinely imaginative, animated and excited for your subject. Aim to get them fascinated with you, the process of hypnotising and the idea of being hypnotized.

2.3 How to tell if someone is hypnotized

If you only give your subject suggestions to relax then the chances are that neither of you will actually know if they are hypnotized or not. In fact if you ask them afterwards they will probably just say that they felt relaxed but do not think they were hypnotized. This is fine if your mutual goal is to show them how to relax. However I am hoping you will want to take it further than that. Even if you suggest things that draw every type of hypnotic phenomena out of them, they are still likely to say to you they were not hypnotized. This is because there is no such feeling as being hypnotized. Remember, your subject is going to act on your suggestions unconsciously. So as far as they are concerned they are completely normal in every way. So there is no point looking to your subject for verification of whether they are hypnotized.

So how do you tell if someone is hypnotized?

By far the easiest way is to give the subject a suggestion and see if they follow it. Instantly and to the letter would be great. In other words test your work. If they appear to be responding then give another suggestion and so on.

It is also useful to develop an 'eye' for the signs of hypnosis, so you can spot who has gone even before you start giving directions that require an obvious physical or emotional response. Someone can be hypnotized and exhibit none of the following signs but many will do so, so watch out for them. They are useful when you are planning to select one or two participants from a group because you can have an insight into who your best subjects might be.

- Eyelids flickering and fluttering - this is the same REM eye movement observed when someone is dreaming. Often this is quite pronounced in the hypnotized subject and it should be encouraged as you can then suggest it will increase and it does.
- Temperature rise - a change in blood flow can be quite visible in some people, depending on their skin tone. It is a useful sign that their state has changed.

- Eyes rolling back up in the head - if you do not see it happen you may spot the whites of their eyes as their eyelids flicker. Some inductions start with the eyes rolled back up in the head. In this position it is very difficult for the subject to open their eyes.
- Breathing shift – sometimes it speeds up but most often the breathing becomes deeper and very steady, similar to when someone is sleeping peacefully.
- Increased lacrimentation – more moisture in and around the eyes. If the eyes are open they may appear glazed.
- Heavy head – with the slightest encouragement, such as gently pushing the head forward, a subjects neck can be relaxed and then it becomes quite difficult to lift the head.

As well as just looking for these signs to assess if your subject is gone, it is also useful to use them to enhance their trance. Inductions can be used that artificially create one of the signs of hypnosis as the method used to hypnotize. You could hypnotize someone by getting them to breathe in for a count of 7 and out for a count of 11, using their count or flow of breath as the focus of attention. You can push your subjects head forward as you say 'sleep'. You can make the focal point of a fixation induction a point inside the head, with the eyes closed and the eyes rolled back.

You can also link one of these signs to the development of another or the acceleration of hypnotic phenomena. For example if you notice that the subject is exhibiting lots of REM then you can bring this into their awareness and create a link between it and the next thing you want to happen.

As your eyes flicker, your hand is getting lighter and lighter and lifting upward.

Most of these signs will be outside the conscious awareness of your subject until you bring their attention to them. So if you notice them you can suggest that they will occur. For example suggest that the subject will begin to feel warmer or that their eyes will flicker. Then when they notice that they are occurring they attribute that to the influence of The Hypnotist and the phenomena will increase. This is probably because the subject begins auto suggesting 'I am getting warmer, am I looking warmer, how does he know I am getting warmer' or 'my eyes are flickering, I can't stop them flickering. I must be hypnotized'. This unconscious panic creates a feedback loop driven by their own internal dialogue. Encourage natural signs of any hypnotic phenomena. Build on them. Develop an eye for them. When you have a group of people and are looking for one of them to work with then use those who exhibit signs of hypnosis and those who look fascinated and keen.

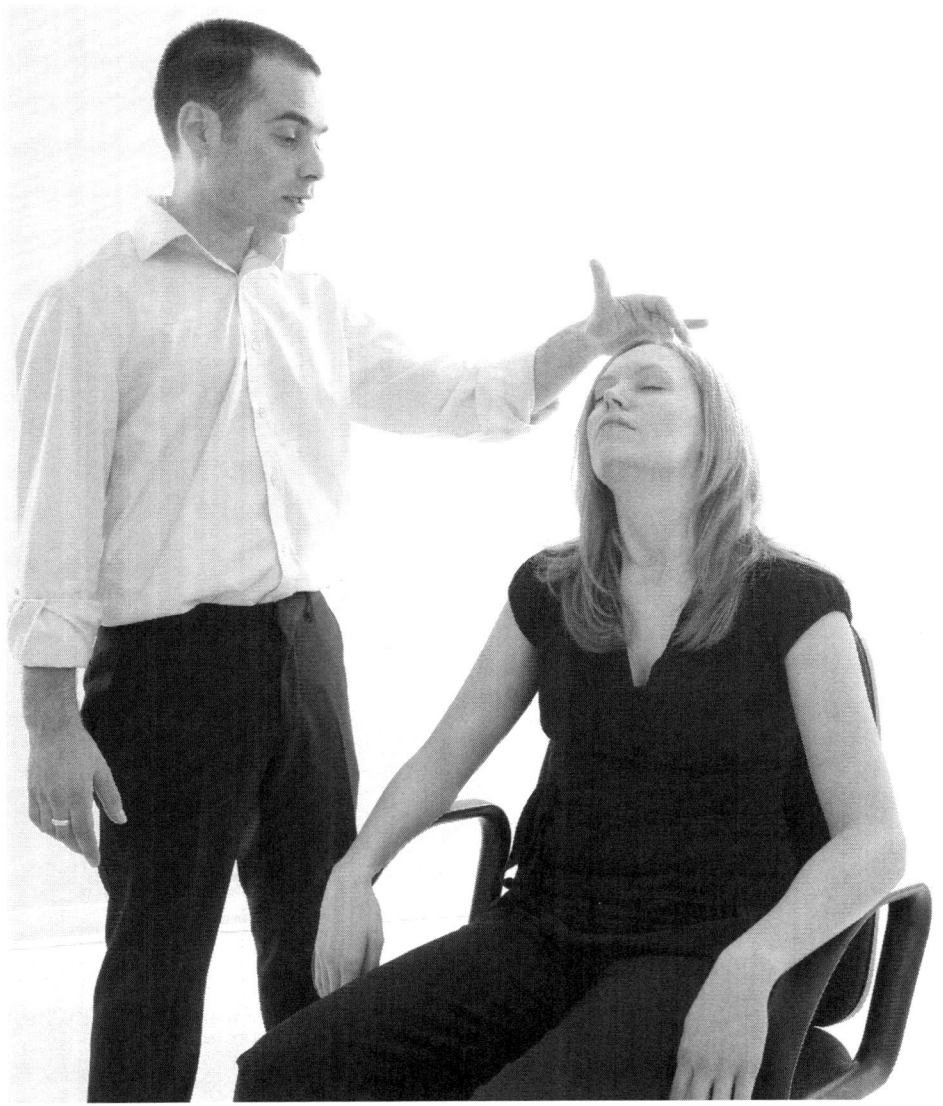

2.4 Hypnotic phenomena.

Once you have someone hypnotized there are a number of phenomena they can experience.
These are:

Catalepsy
Loss of conscious control of the ability to move part of the body. Lack of response to external stimuli and muscle rigidity

Ideomotor Movements
Unconscious movements, like the head nodding, fingers twitching and legs shaking.

Amnesia
Inability to recall information or loss of memory.

Hallucinations of all Senses
Sensing something that is not there or not sensing something that is.

Dissociation
Separation of mind and body.

Hypermnesia
Improved recall.

Regression
Reversion to earlier or more infantile patterns of behaviour and memory.

Revivification
Recall and re-experience of a past event.

Analgesia
Partial sensory loss.

Anaesthesia
Total sensory loss.

Time Distortion
Contraction and expansion of the perception of time.

Catalepsy is one of the foremost examples of hypnotic phenomena, well documented and used in many ways – a classic in the field. First described by Charcot, in 1882 it is a useful and versatile hypnotic tool (8). If you have put someone in a trance and you reach over and lift up his or her arm, you will probably find it is cataleptic and will just float there – it stays where you put it rather than dropping down as you might expect. It is often combined with surprise or instant inductions of hypnosis and hence looks dramatic. Many of the inductions in this book encourage catalepsy. The key is being able to arrest someone's attention in such a way or for long enough that they forget that arm or hand. They forget how it feels normally and may begin to auto suggest. It is at the very minimum a useful sign that you have induced trance and a useful convincer for the subject that something has occurred. Beyond this it can be used to move to other more advanced hypnotic phenomena and used as a way of encouraging ideomotor communication directly with the unconscious mind and body without the need for verbal responses.

Catalepsy is a physiological condition where balanced tonicity exists between the agonist and antagonist muscles. In plain English that means it stays in a certain position. Muscles that are used to move a body part usually have another 'opposite' that enables you to move it back again. The bicep and tricep on the upper arm for example. When these opposite numbers are balanced the body part does not move. One pair in your body that are working all the time you are awake are in your neck. They are keeping your head up.

When catalepsy is induced in hypnosis and combined with ideomotor movement to make someone lift their arm, the feelings, the kinaesthetics and proprioceptive sense are both quite different from those you experience when you lift your arm voluntarily. Watch someone's arm lift cataleptically and you will see it is a bit like a possessed movement in a horror movie – like a winch is lifting it. "Waxy flexibility" is a great term for describing the feeling and well known psychiatric term for describing catatonia (9). This is also something you can bring to your subjects attention.

You can notice your arm lifting and notice it is moving in kind of jerky reflex movements. That is because your unconscious is lifting your arm. It allows your conscious mind to lift it smoothly but your unconscious moves it in this more reflex like way.

Catatonia is a term for catatonic schizophrenic patients who live in a permanent state of catalepsy – you can move them however you want and they stay in the position you leave them in. Years ago I saw a street performer mimic this condition. He stood on a box that had the words 'Move me' written on the front. You put some money down and could move him into any position you wished and he would stay there until someone else came along and moved him. It is quite straightforward to provoke catalepsy in your hypnotized subject. Understand that a hand on the arm of a chair can be cataleptic; it does not need to be floating in the air, just outside of conscious control.

In the therapy room catalepsy can be used as an advanced form of ideomotor signalling - using catalepsy and subsequent movements of the body as a line of communication. An arm may lift higher for a yes signal, perhaps one arm for yes and one arm for no.

Ernst Rossi uses ideomotor signalling as a way of communicating with the subject's deep unconscious intelligence in the body (10).

For the purposes of impromptu hypnosis become an expert at getting your subject to develop catalepsy. It is useful for many things including:

- Convincing - demonstrate the unconscious is at play – the subject is hypnotized.
- Inducing trance – use it as a Set Piece or the induction itself.
- As a routine – turn them into a coat rack or a statue.
- Communicating - ideomotor signals.
- Leverage - to springboard to other hypnotic phenomena.

When using catalepsy you could either induce trance first and then suggest eye, hand, arm or full body catalepsy or incorporate creating catalepsy as part of the trance induction itself. All of the methods in section three that include catalepsy can be used as a hypnotic induction rather than just The Set Piece. Once your subject has achieved catalepsy they are highly suggestible.

If you have made it impossible for your subject to move their arm then encourage them to try and move it. Encourage them to really try and put all their effort into it. Tell them they can try but their unconscious is a superpower and it is working for them. The realisation that they are clearly more than they thought they were before they came in to see you is a beautiful one and an experience that will stay with them. At the very least they will have something to say when asked what happened when they went to see the hypnotist. For many it is quite a mind-blowing experience. If they are really getting into it encourage them to open their eyes and look at the part of the body you have made cataleptic. Ask them if it belongs to them. When a subject has their eyes open such a challenge to try and move their arm seems to be made even more potent. Many people will get a little agitated at this point, instruct them to close their eyes, let them know it might feel peculiar but they will enjoy it, and go even deeper as you bomb them with more directions. Their mind is wide open at that point and ready to receive.

3.0 The Set Piece

What follows are a number of physical and psychological manipulations
– individually or collectively they can be thought of as The Set Piece. They are
your first rung on the hypnotic ladder and should be learnt well and understood.
The techniques are classics of hypnosis but often their value is overlooked. If
you have already come across them please revisit them.

The techniques described in this section are all well known and have been used
by hypnotists for decades and are often referred to as 'tests of suggestibility'
or exercises in 'waking hypnosis' (11). Both of these descriptions sell these
techniques short. They can be used with groups of people just as readily as one
to one. Generally they are used before the real induction of hypnosis begins.
There are many good reasons why The Hypnotist should be able to confidently
do a Set Piece. So learn them well. Understand the principles and applications.
Use them.

- Set Pieces are often thought of and used as tests of how responsive to
  suggestion the subject is. In other words a gauge of how good, willing
  and able to be hypnotized they are.
- The Set Piece gives The Hypnotist an opportunity to observe the
  subject under direction, gather information and assess their suitability as
  a subject.
- Just as importantly it gives the subject an opportunity to experience
  The Hypnotists power of suggestion and influence and their own ability
  to cooperate. If the subject experiences something they consider out of
  the ordinary they gain confidence in both the skill of the hypnotist and
  their own ability to be hypnotized - they let go and become more
  fascinated with the process. Likewise the hypnotist gains confidence in
  the subject.
- The Set Piece fires up the imagination, focuses attention and builds
  expectation in the subject that they are about to be hypnotized or are
  being hypnotized.
- Finally The Set Piece can be used as the induction into hypnosis rather
  than just as a pre-runner to it. This is perhaps the most powerful and
  overlooked application.

Some hypnotists do not use these techniques. One reason given is that if the subject fails to do what is asked of them then it is more difficult to hypnotize them – this is true to some extent, especially if The Set Piece is presented as a 'test'. As your ultimate aim is to hypnotize the subject to accept your suggestions it is important to see if they are receptive to simple ones early on. Certainly failing a test is not helpful but it is not the end of the world either. It just passes by as a non event by the subject unless the hypnotist gets in a fluster about it. Most people will pass the exercises very easily and if they cannot then it might be wise to pick another subject or take an entirely different approach. There really is no need to present these The Set Piece as a tests. That way there is no possibility of failure. It is fine to simply say 'Let's try something' or 'Let me show you something interesting' or call them an 'exercise in concentration' and proceed.

Another reason they are overlooked or used in a limited fashion is that many of the techniques have some physiological/mechanical reason why they work – the odds are stacked that the subject will succeed – so some hypnotists believe they are being dishonest in using them or just miss their value and dismiss them as tricks. This is missing the point. Just use them and any other trick necessary to excite the imagination.

Deliver The Set Piece with a tone that is bright and upbeat, a manner that is confident and commanding and generally move along at a fairly rapid pace. Find your own way and ensure that your attitude communicates that you are confident, knowledgeable and expecting to hypnotize.

It is also important that your subject does not see The Set Piece as something they should be trying to battle or resist. Equally you do not want them to pretend. Make sure they understand this. For example if you were going to ask them to imagine their hands were like magnets so that they come together and touch automatically you can say this.

I don't want you to push them together or try to keep them apart, I just want you to concentrate, imagine your hands are magnets and your body will respond.

If they follow your instructions, concentrate on the ideas you are presenting and genuinely use their imagination then they are very likely to do well in The Set Piece and be set up perfectly for the hypnotic induction itself.

3.1 Magnetic Fingers

In this exercise you are going to make the index fingers of your subject move together like magnets.

OK, let's try something. A simple exercise to fire up your power of concentration. I'd like you to place your hands out in front of you like this.

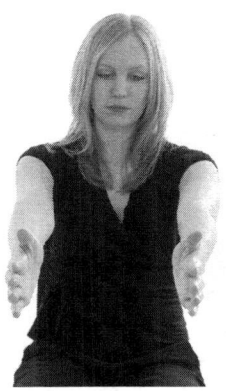 

Now can you clasp your hands together, palms together and thumbs crossed, nice and tight.

Now bend your elbows like you are making a desperate prayer. You can make one while you are there if you like. Now put your first fingers, your index fingers, straight up, about an inch apart.

Now look at the gap between those fingers, not my fingers just at your fingers, and concentrate, because in a moment your fingers will come together and touch, just like they are magnets, that's it, they are starting to twitch, closer and closer and as soon as those fingers touch you can allow your eyes to close and relax.

Open your eyes. Brilliant that shows me you can concentrate.

Ninety nine percent of people will do this successfully – you should aim to get their fingers together swiftly, as quickly as 2 seconds and no more than 20 seconds. If they cannot do it within this time, do something else. The reason this exercise is so easy to succeed in is that the effect of the fingers moving without conscious effort is heavily reliant on the physiology of the hands. Try it out and this time squeeze your hands together as you watch your fingers. As the tendons in the other fingers tighten it causes the tendons in the index fingers to tighten and they come together quite automatically.

The most common presentation of this exercise involves a demonstration and explanation of what is going to happen and a request to 'squeeze the hands and all of the fingers together except the index fingers.'

In most cases you will get away with this approach. However it does make it kind of obvious that some physiological principle is at play. So to avoid making it so obvious do not mention squeezing the hands. Just use suggestion. Do what you are purporting to do and make it happen with your powers of suggestion and influence. Be The Hypnotist, this is often your first real chance to do something with your subject, make it count.

You will see from the scripting above that the tension is placed into the hands in the set-up. This is important because if the subject just has the fingers loosely interlocked it is much less likely they will succeed, so ensure that they follow your instructions. If they have not, then say it again making it absolutely clear what you want them to do. Demonstrate with your own hands as you go through the instructions. Then as soon as the hands are set-up there should be a change of pace and a direct suggestion from The Hypnotist about what is going to happen.

...because in a moment your fingers will come together and touch, just like they are powerful magnets.

You should up the tempo and forcefulness of your delivery at this point.

When using this technique and any other Set Piece exercise, even if you know the odds are stacked in your favour, your mind set as The Hypnotist should be that you are making this happen. Then you will be congruent and convincing in your approach. Your words and actions will create the effect.

Although simple and easy to dismiss as a schoolboy trick you will be surprised at just how much some subjects react to this test. Wide eyed expressions and exclamations of surprise that what you are saying will happen is happening are common.

Immediately you can go into a stronger test, such as Magnetic Hands or Stiff Arm. Or you can proceed immediately with an induction.

3.2 Magnetic Hands

In this exercise you are going to make the hands of your subject move together as if they were magnets.

Now in a moment I will ask you to concentrate just like you did on your fingers only this time I want you to really use your imagination so in a moment I will ask you to close your eyes. I'll ask you to place your hands out in front of you like this, to close your eyes and imagine you have two powerful magnets strapped to the palms of your hands pulling them together. When they touch, your head can simply fall forward as you relax.

OK, so place your hands out in front of you; look at the space between those hands, get a clear picture of your hands stuck out there, now close your eyes and imagine you have two powerful magnets strapped to the palms of your hands pulling them together.

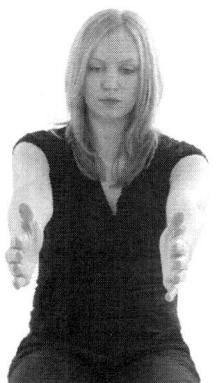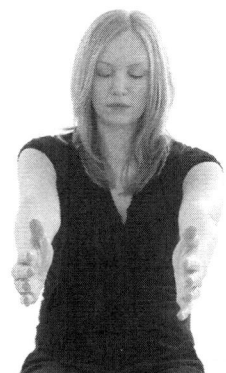
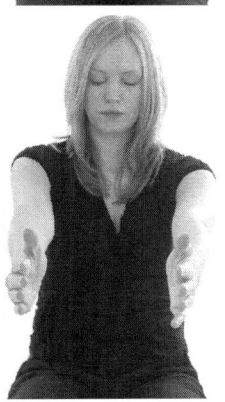

They are already starting to go, imagine that magnetic force is getting stronger, the closer they get the stronger it becomes, just like when as a child playing with magnets you felt that magnetic attraction, pulling those hands together. I know it is difficult to tell exactly when they are going to touch but I can assure you they are going to touch. Now let your hands drop down as your head drops forward onto your chest and relax.

Excellent. Now open your eyes you have a powerful imagination.

In this exercise I suggest The Hypnotist demonstrates exactly what the subject has to do and what will happen before asking the subject to do it. Once you have explained what is going to happen and demonstrated it happening it is highly likely the subject will succeed at this exercise – even more so if they have passed the Magnetic Fingers exercise.

Magnetic Hands logically follows Magnetic Fingers as again it involves 'magnetic' forces and parts of the body moving automatically – without conscious effort. It also builds upon the subjects successful demonstration that they can concentrate by asking them to concentrate again and use their imagination. The exercise can be done with the eyes open. However in saying 'This time I want you to really use your imagination so in a moment I will ask you to close your eyes' you are giving the subject a reason to close their eyes and this gives you an opportunity to observe them responding to your suggestions with closed eyes and makes it easier for them to use their imagination. At this point you can observe them closely for any signs of hypnosis, especially REM.

A traditional approach to hypnotic induction was to suggest the eyes would get heavy and close. This is fine, if a little slow. So give them a reason to close them instead and then do something more interesting.

Magnetic Hands is a stronger test of their powers of concentration and imagination than Magnetic Fingers because there is much less reliance on the mechanics of the body and much more emphasis on suggestion. There is of course some mechanics involved. If you place the hands out in front of you as they tire they begin to drop and naturally fall inwards. However just as with the finger exercise it is important that you as The Hypnotist make this happen, want it to happen and expect it to happen.

Think of the subjects arms as your arms. They do what you tell them to do. Take ownership of them like they are two objects entirely detached from the subject.

When the hands touch you again have an opportunity to link what they have achieved to something else. This could simply be an opportunity to let the subject know they can relax or are doing well and will go into hypnosis easily. It could be that as they touch their head will drop forward and they will go to into a deep sleep. The choice is yours.

3.3 Stiff Arm

In this exercise you are going to make the arm of your subject stiff so that they cannot bend it.

I present this in one of two ways. The first is done from an eyes open conversational state much like Magnetic Fingers and Magnetic Hands. The second approach is done when you already have the subject with eyes closed. This might be following Magnetic Hands – rather than getting them to open their eyes you just get straight into the Stiff Arm. Sometimes I use this after I have done the actual hypnotic induction. In that sense it is an early routine.

<u>Method one</u> - Firstly you need to get permission to take hold of your subjects arm. Always get permission from your subject if you are going to touch them. Straighten their arm out in front of them.

Give me your arm. Now make a tight fist and the muscles tense.

Slap the palm of your hand on their fist and poke their muscles with your finger as you say the following.

Even tighter in your forearm, your tricep, right into your shoulder. Imagine you have a steel bar running through your fist through your elbow to the shoulder, your arm is like a steel bar.

Now your arm is getting stiff… make it stiff, stiff… stiffer and stiffer, tighter and tighter…you cannot bend it try as hard as you will. Try hard and find you cannot bend it, the harder you try the stiffer it gets. You cannot bend your arm.

Once the subject has tried in vain to bend their arm you can remove the effect easily by just touching their arm and saying the following.

All right, it is all gone now. You can bend your arm now. It is loose and relaxed and normal in every way.

Method two – Your subject is sitting with their hands in their lap and their eyes closed waiting for your next instruction perhaps following Magnetic Hands.

I am going to count from one to three. On the count of one I want you to make a tight fist with your right hand. On two, I want you to raise that arm up toward the ceiling and on three to really make that fist as tight as you can. One, make that fist, two, raise it up toward the ceiling now three make that fist, tight and feel that stiffness, feel the skin on the back of the hand tightening, the wrist locking out.

Even tighter in your forearm, your tricep, right into your shoulder.

Imagine you have a steel bar running through your fist, through your elbow to the shoulder, your arm is like a steel bar.

Now you arm is getting stiff... make it stiff, stiff... stiffer and stiffer, tighter and tighter...you cannot bend it try as hard as you will. Try hard and find you cannot bend it, the harder you try the stiffer it gets. You cannot bend your arm.

This kind of Set Piece is normally met with a slightly baffled but amused response by the subject.

Again there is a physiological reason why the Stiff Arm works. You are simultaneously asking your subject to tense their arm and to try and bend it. Clearly if they take the first instruction they will be unable to carry out the second. However the effect it has on the mind is very real. Do not dismiss this as a pseudo hypnosis trick. Instead use it to trip your subject into hypnosis.

If you cannot bend your own arm or keep your hands from moving or open your eyes despite your best efforts then it is clear that the conscious critical mind is bypassed.

Sometimes when you actually step up to the challenge the work you have done by saying 'Try and bend it', the arm will start to bend a little. Even at that point continue with your suggestions. Remind them that it feels stiff and will straighten out or set into place. There is no point snatching defeat from the jaws of victory.

In any Set Piece it is important that what the subject is being asked to do is not objectionable. Presenting these exercises as a demonstration of the subject's ability to concentrate and use their imagination is not objectionable. So take the opportunity to congratulate them, flatter them and encourage them. The subjects mind is easily locked around a single idea.

4.0 Inductions

Induction is the generic term used to describe the process or technique used to put someone into hypnosis. There are thousands of ways of doing this. Although being flexible in your approach is desirable, you will be more effective by being extremely accomplished at one or two inductions rather than simply knowing lots of them. Many people continue to seek out new inductions as if they believe there must be more to it or if they could just find the ultimate induction they would then be a great hypnotist. Ultimately it is The Hypnotist that does the hypnotising, not the technique itself. Some inductions are direct, some indirect. An induction can be rapid, instant or slow and progressive. They can be overt or covert, verbal or non verbal. The inductions outlined here are all rapid, overt, verbal and physical inductions.

Bear in mind that if your subject has done well in The Set Piece then they may already be hypnotized or well on their way. Although Elman suggests that this is the just the entering wedge, my experience is that as soon as you have got some success with The Set Piece then you are one suggestion away from hypnosis. If you have suggested the subjects arm will not bend and they cannot bend it then they have already bypassed their critical faculty and established selective thinking around at least one idea – the idea that their arm will not bend. Their unconscious is seemingly receptive to the ideas you are presenting to it.

This is why The Set Piece can be the induction itself. If the subjects arm is unbendable because you suggested it would be and you suddenly push it down and direct the subject to 'Sleep!' they probably will go straight into hypnosis and simply wait for your next instruction. It is up to you whether you use it that way or not. Even if after making the subjects arm unbendable you were to just touch it and say 'OK, you can bend your arm now, it is normal', in your head you can still assume the subject is in the state of mind you want them to be in. It may not have occurred to them that they are hypnotized or even that the hypnotising has begun. In this sense the induction that follows The Set Piece is a way of intensifying their state of hypnosis rather than creating it. More on that in Section 5.

The following inductions are all rapid – meaning they take anything from a few seconds to a few minutes to perform. They generally involve some physical manipulation of your subject – this could mean taking control of their eyes, arm, wrist, hand, head or balance. This rapid approach is the most effective for impromptu applications of hypnosis. It could be argued that it is the most effective for hypnosis full stop – wherever or for whatever purpose it is used.

They assume rapport has been established and that you are already pacing and beginning to lead your client through the Set Up. More often than not I have already been through The Set Piece by the time I do an induction. That said, The Set Piece is not required prior to using any of these inductions. However it makes your work easier if you have used a Set Piece. It could be you have just been introduced to someone as a Hypnotist and they have expressed an interest in being hypnotized and you want to get straight into it. It could be that you are not announcing you are The Hypnotist and just springing the induction on an unsuspecting subject to be. You will find these inductions are flexible and can be adapted to suit all circumstances.

Confidence, certainty and a matter of fact attitude that the person will go into a trance go a long way to using these techniques successfully. Some hypnotists get this right from the start others have to do their best to develop this character.

4.1 The Rehearsal

This generic rehearsal induction has been used for many years in hypnosis (12). It was the first impromptu rapid induction I learnt and it worked superbly. It is great for the fledgling hypnotist because it allows you to practise on the subject before doing the 'real induction'. I have never failed to hypnotize using this induction and I still use it when I think it is appropriate.

You explain to your subject in a step-by-step fashion exactly what you are going to say and do and what affect it will have on them. Present it in a matter of fact tone as if you are trying to teach them something.

This version uses rehearsal to create catalepsy in their arm. You literally rehearse, as many times as required until it is time for the 'real' induction. Strangely you will never make it to the 'real' induction. The subject will become hypnotized during one of the rehearsals, hence the name.

Can I borrow your arm?

What I'm going to do here in a moment is I'm just going to reach over like this, and I'm going to pick up your hand, and I don't want you to go into hypnosis, because I want to explain this to you...

As you say this pick up the hand of the subject by the wrist and move it up so that their hand is in the air and their elbow bent at about 90 degrees.

 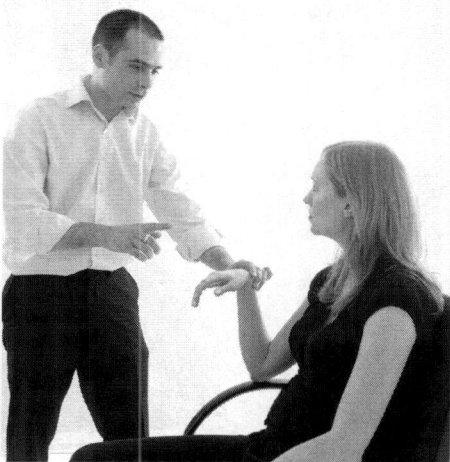

…because this is something that will help you later on in getting hypnotized…and then to have you come back out of hypnosis we are going to move that hand back down like that.

As you say this move their hand back down.

All you are going to notice is that I'm going to pick up your wrist like this.

Pick up wrist and speaking more softly but still at a regular conversational pace.

I'm going to talk to you in a certain way and as that hand reaches a certain point, you'll notice a number of things happening that will let you know you're going into hypnosis…your eyes close, your breathing will shift and you would go even deeper, and then to have you come back out, wide awake, we'll move the hand back down like this. OK?

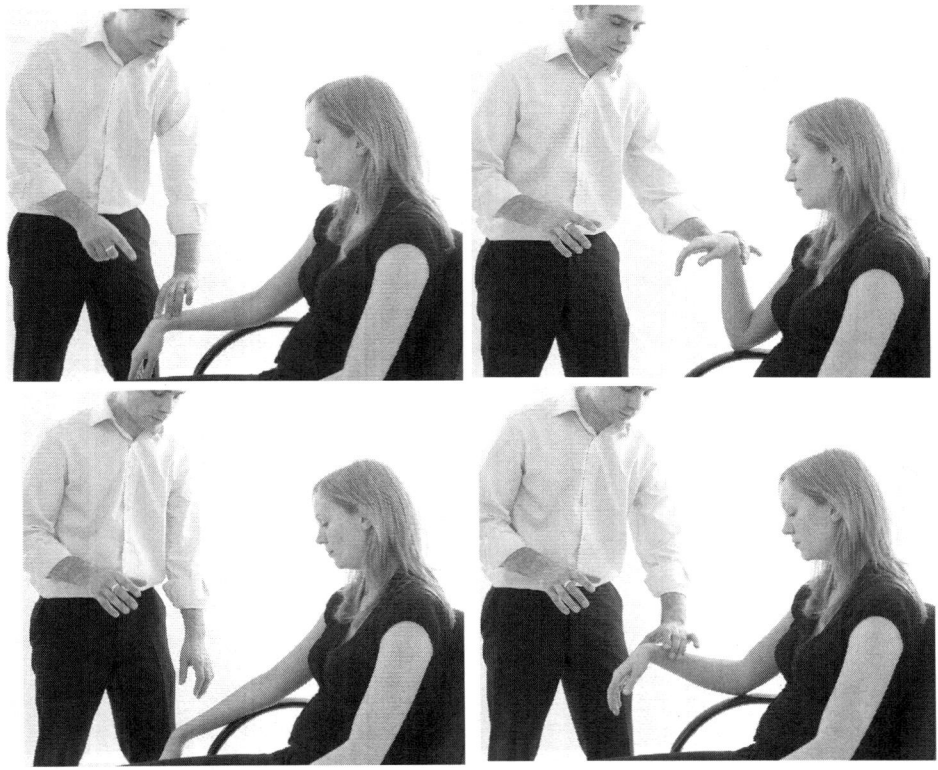

So I am not going to do it yet, I just want you to get the feeling, so if now's the time to do it, all I would do is reach over like this, I would pick your arm up like that and stop at a point when you would go inside, probably notice then that your eyes would close at a certain point, it's going to stop all by itself. Then I'm going to move it back down. OK.

You have just added a few steps, small details. Begin pacing and leading their experience. In other words point out to them what is happening and ambiguously suggest what is going to happen all the time looking for any signs of hypnosis developing and building that into your patter.

Now if we were actually going to do it again, all I would do is reach over.

It is likely on the third or fourth time that you go to lift their arm that it will start to lift up before you even touch it. What occurs as you rehearse is you train their arm to respond. This is what you want. When it does all you do is give it the minimal amount of encouragement upwards with your thumb on the underside of their wrist as you concentrate on them developing the other signs that they are going into hypnosis.

And as that arm lifts, like that, as your eyes close, and when that arm stops by itself.

Their arm will probably remain suspended now even if you let go, I tend to slowly release all of the fingers except for the index finger on the back of their wrist. This gives the message that the hand is still being held in some way and if it is not cataleptic already means that you can manipulate it a little more if required.

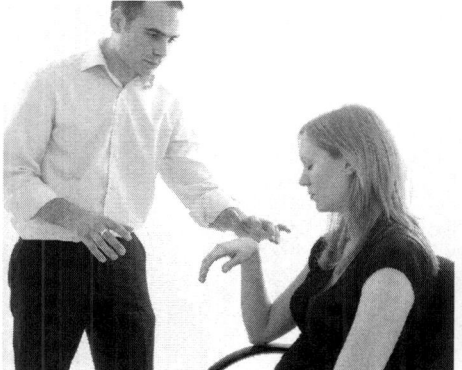 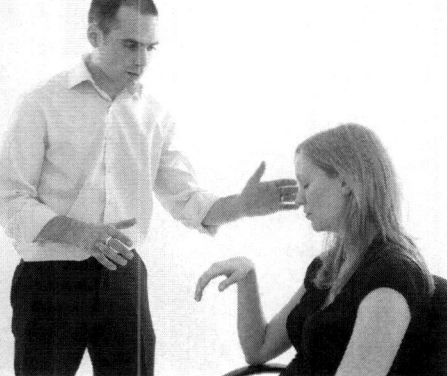

And you know what to do, all the way in…that's right…eyes closed, deep asleep, deep asleep. And your unconscious mind can follow exquisitely the suggestions with your conscious mind paying attention or going anywhere it wishes.

Now the question is how deeply into a trance can you go? How much deeper can you go? That's right….arm lifting now, even higher…that's right.

If their eyes are still open say the following to direct them to close.

I want you to watch, stay awake even more focus until it's time…that's right…eyes closed now all the way into a deep state.

Proceed to deepen the trance or simply give a hypnotic suggestion and bring the hand down only as quickly as it is needed.

That's right I don't want that hand to drift down to your lap only as quickly as you can drift down, all the way down, remaining in that trance, the muscles relax you can relax as that arm drifts down you can drift down. Deeper and deeper to sleep.

From that point on you can go wherever you wish to. There is no need for any further induction.

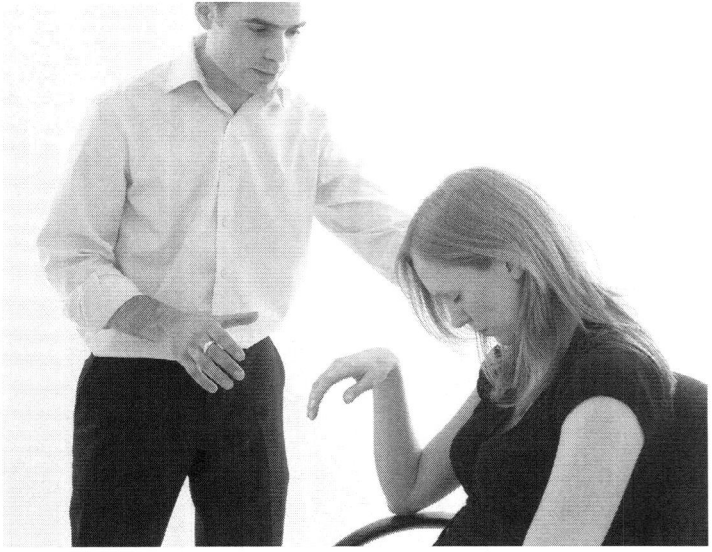

4.2 Eye to Hand Fixation

This induction is simple, fast and flexible. It is the one I use the most. It involves The Hypnotist showing someone their own hand and fixating their gaze upon it. I tend to use the palm of the hand but the back of the hand will do. Depending on how the chairs are positioned I use either of my hands on either of theirs. If you plan to use this approach you could adjust the seating to suit you. There is no need to be concerned about hemispheric dominance. Just lift their arm up by the wrist to a position they would naturally adopt if inspecting their own palm. The palm should be about 30 cm from their face. Watch their eyes to make sure that they are zoned in on one spot. If they are scanning around their entire hand or looking at you every now and again that is no good. Looking at a spot will focus and narrow their attention. Continue to hold their wrist with a light touch, adjusting your fingertips to encourage their arm to take its own weight. Then move it toward their face and pace their experience.

In a moment, if it is OK with you I would like to borrow your arm. I am going to pick your hand up by the wrist. Is that OK?

Great, give me your arm. Just find a spot on your hand you can look at and keep looking at that spot. Ready?

Don't look at the whole thing just keep your eyes on one spot, that's it.

Some arms will have absolutely no weight at all. They had probably gone into hypnosis before you took hold of their wrist.

Some arms are really heavy and you will take all the weight. Bob those hands around in front of their chest for a bit and wait until you feel the arm lock in place. You should feel it 'go'. As you move it up and down into 'position' with a light touch it will suddenly support itself. If you keep your index finger on the outside edge of their wrist you can test it supports itself by just maintaining contact with that finger. The subject cannot quite tell if you are supporting it or not and this encourages them to dissociate from their hand and arm.

If it has not locked in place after a little while (10 seconds) just remind them to focus their attention on that spot. Have positive meaningful expectancy sewn into your approach. Hold it as a core belief of yours that they are a great hypnotic subject. Expect their arm to lock in place.

That's right keep your eyes on that spot.

As that hand begins to move toward your face, your eyes will begin to change focus and as you become aware of those eyes.

You have choices about how to proceed from this point.

Most often I will simply pass my hand in a downward motion past their eyes as I tell them to close them and say the following.

Close your eyes and sleep now. In a moment I'm going to count down from 3 to zero and as I count down from 3 to zero your hand will float back down to your lap your head will fall forward onto your chest and you will go so much deeper into the trance. 3 - 2 - 1 - 0. Deep asleep. All the way down. Deep, deep, deeper asleep.

Then continue to deepen or test your work by giving them further direction.

Or I leave their eyes open and say,

That's right, with your eyes open, fixed on that point; understand that you have an incredibly powerful unconscious mind. Much stronger than your conscious mind. In a moment I'm going to touch the back of your hand and when I touch the back of your hand your unconscious is going to start pulling it towards your face. Now you could pretend that, but that's not what I want. So when I touch the back of your hand and you feel it start to pull, you can try and stop it. Just like those hands were magnets, you will find your head is a magnet and that hand is a magnet. You can try and stop it lifting higher and find you cannot. You're a strong man/woman. Really try to stop it happening and let's see just how much stronger your unconscious is.

Then touch the hand. On its way to their face, usually with a good deal of shaking going on in their upper body as they fight with their own arm, you can encourage more futile resistance.

You're a strong woman, try even harder and find it lifts higher, the harder you try the more difficult it becomes.

You can use the arrival of the hand at the face as the trigger for the deepening of trance.

When your hand touches your face your eyes will close and you will go so much deeper into the hypnosis. Profound hypnosis. Complete physical and mental bliss.

4.3 Magnetic Palms

Hypnotists have used this simple technique for decades. It is a great group induction. It will pull your subjects hands together like magnets and if you wish stick their hands together. Good fun when at a party or down the pub but also very useful in the therapy room. Although technically it barely differs from its use as a Set Piece, here it is used as a rapid induction. It is useful for you because it gives the subject an experience of their ability, to affect their body with their mind, sets up the promotion of catalepsy, creates a moment of wonder or confusion, demonstrates hypnotic phenomena and demonstrates your position as The Hypnotist.

Have you ever been hypnotized before?

If they have then great. There is less need to explain anything and you can use their experience if it was a good one. If not then just ignore their answer, let them know they will find this interesting and move on.

What do you think hypnosis is?

After thinking for a moment the subject will likely say, relaxation, sleep or something else. Whatever they say immediately counter with the following, or something similar, that matches up to what they have said.

That's right it is all about using your mind. I would like you to do something for me. It might feel a little strange at first, but I can assure you everything will return to normal afterwards, if you don't feel something, you don't feel something, it takes a little while, but just relax and wait for it, it will happen – it is always different with each person as we all think and feel things in different ways.

These opening comments do many things. They suggest something will happen. They suggest it may be a bit odd. They say very little about what the experience will be. You do not have to use them but they are a useful bit of set up (13).

OK are you ready to be hypnotised? Can you put your arms out like this, about shoulder height, palms facing towards each other?
Now in a moment I will ask you to concentrate just like you did on your fingers only this time I want you to really use your imagination so in a moment I will ask you to close your eyes. I'll ask you to place your hands out in front of you like this, to close your eyes and imagine you have two powerful magnets strapped to the palms of your hands pulling them together. When they touch your head can simply fall forward as you relax.

OK, so place your hands out in front of you, look at the space between those hands, and get a clear picture of your hands stuck out there, now close your eyes and imagine you have two powerful magnets strapped to the palms of your hands pulling them together.

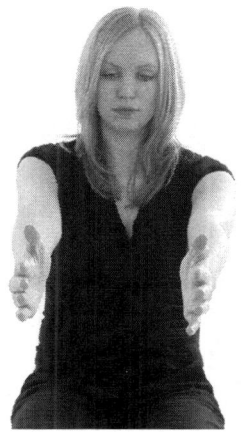 

 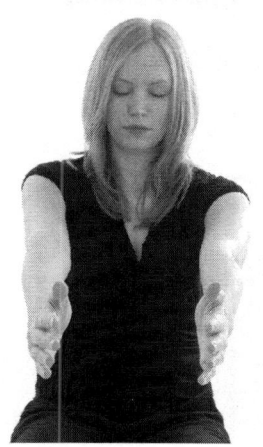

They are already starting to go, imagine that magnetic force is getting stronger, the closer they get the stronger it becomes, I know it is difficult to tell exactly when they are going to touch but I can assure you they are going to touch, just like when as a child, playing with magnets you felt that magnetic attraction, pulling those hands together.

Now let your hands drop down and relax. Sleep.

This closing eyes step is not necessary but I find it helps. It may surprise them when the hands touch. If you keep their eyes open it is also quite surprising when they see their hands moving and tends to fixate their attention, you could then link the moment they touch to eye closure and hypnosis.

4.4 The Handshake

There are various handshake inductions – that is hypnotising someone
with a handshake. Elman outlined a handshake induction. Milton Erickson
developed at least two variations. He is known to have used a handshake as
an opportunity to induce hypnosis so often that rarely would anyone wish
to shake his hand. He would not quite let go of their hand and would use an
ambiguous touch until the hand took its own weight and developed catalepsy.

The technique outlined below is widely credited to Richard Bandler, one of
the co-founders of Neuro Linguistic Programming (NLP) (14).

This is easier to pull off than Erickson's ambiguous touch and I find it is
one of the easiest and most effective rapid inductions. You go to shake the
subjects hand and interrupt the handshake by taking hold of their wrist with
your other hand and showing the palm of their hand to them. This creates a
moment of confusion and you lead the subject into trance. It can all be done
in less than 10 seconds. If it can be used after a Set Piece or done from cold.
It is one of the best inductions for unannounced impromptu hypnosis.

Offer your right hand to the subject (like a handshake) and say something
that encourages them to respond. For example if they have just completed
The Set Piece I may say something like this.

Thanks for doing that.

Or,

Excellent. Can I borrow your hand?

As the subject offers their hand to shake yours, pull your hand away slightly and use your left hand to lightly grasp the subject's right wrist and move their palm to a distance of about 30cm from their face. Point at their hand as you give them their first direction.

Look at your hand.

Continue at a pace speaking with some command.

That's right....just look at that hand, as you watch that hand move towards you.

Move it slightly towards the subjects face while pointing at it with the other hand.

You can notice the changing focus of your eyes and as you do, notice the tendency for your eyes to close.

Simultaneous to the phrase 'eyes to close' drop your pointing hand downward and away from their focus so that there eyes are encouraged to follow. You can snap your fingers to encourage this. You can do both.

Assuming the eyes are closed (or even if they are not) continue.

As you notice that hand is getting closer and closer to your face.

The hand is hopefully moving cataleptically now to the point where you could let go of it and it would continue to move.

That's right closer and closer (slow down and soften voice and delivery)**... until you just allow it to happen...all the way...down...that's right...all the way down while that hands remains totally fixed there right there.**

The subject is now in a light trance with a cataleptic arm. It is up to you whether you wish to continue deepening trance or just use the existing situation to deliver some other suggestions.

So what is happening in the handshake induction above?

The key ingredient to making this move a success is often touted as successfully interrupting the automatic motor program associated with handshaking. It is common for someone to automatically respond to an outstretched hand offering a handshake by sticking out their hand and completing the shake. It is an unconscious move on their part because it is something we are trained to do from childhood. When you interrupt this pattern, by seizing the wrist rather than actually shaking hands, conscious activity is temporarily suspended while they search for meaning in the interruption. They are looking for the next cue about how to proceed – wait too long, more than a second or two being too long, and they will find it themselves – but if you make use of this window by going straight into the script above you can keep them suspended there.

The way you do that is to pace exactly what occurs starting with the move toward the face. Of course the eyes will change focus as this occurs; of course they will close at some point. So the technique paces these two things and then leads them to 'sleep'

Success with this induction is directly proportional to you feeling confident they will go into a trance. Move swiftly after the pattern interrupt, project confidence and trance will ensue. Go and find a traffic warden or someone pestering you with a questionnaire in the street and practice.

From personal experience I find the emphasis on the pattern interrupt element of the handshake induction often prevents people from using it. In truth you can use it without shock, surprise or confusion. It still works. Used in this way the hand is just a fixation point that you use to send them into hypnosis much like the Eye to Hand Fixation uses a spot on the palm of the hand. This is actually one of the easier inductions to do. Master it.

4.5 Jacquin Power Lift

This induction combines confusion, rehearsal, a pattern interrupt and creates catalepsy. It is my father Freddy Jacquin's, wonderful creation. He is a renowned hypnotherapist and has probably hypnotised over 30,000 people, a large proportion of them using this induction. It is rapid and direct and reliable and flexible. It can be used one to one or with small groups in any setting. Like all of these rapid inductions success is reliant on your intent and expectation not the technique itself. This is our preferred induction especially if the subject is seated or standing at a bar – basically somewhere their elbow can be supported, although it can also be done without elbow support.

OK, I'm going to take you into a trance. I am going to show you what I am going to do then I am going to do it.

Point at their hand and say the following.

In a moment I am going to reach over and pick up that hand, and as I lift it up like this.

Demonstrate by reaching over with the thumb and first two fingers of one hand, taking hold of your wrist lifting your own arm into the Red Indian HOW sign.

As it lifts to about here I want you to allow your eyes to close.

Close your eyes to further demonstrate what you want them to do.

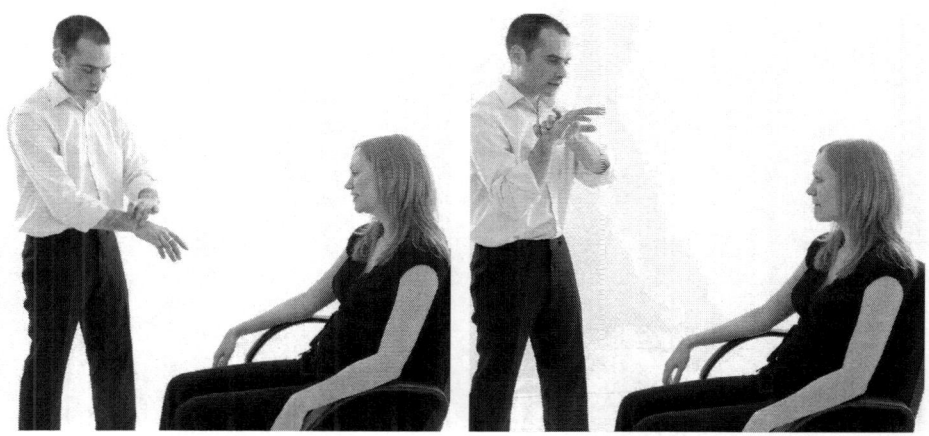

As I push it down (demonstrate) **your eyes will open and you can just relax.**

Demonstrate again by opening your eyes as the hand moves down. Then give a second demonstration.

Then as I pull your arm up your eyes WILL close, as I push it down your eyes will open and you will relax even more.

Is that OK with you? So can I borrow your arm?

Reach over and pick the arm up by the wrist bending the elbow. There is no need to pull it up immediately, perhaps pause a moment or two, to look for any of the signs of hypnosis as they begin to focus inwards.

As I lift it up you can allow your eyes to close.

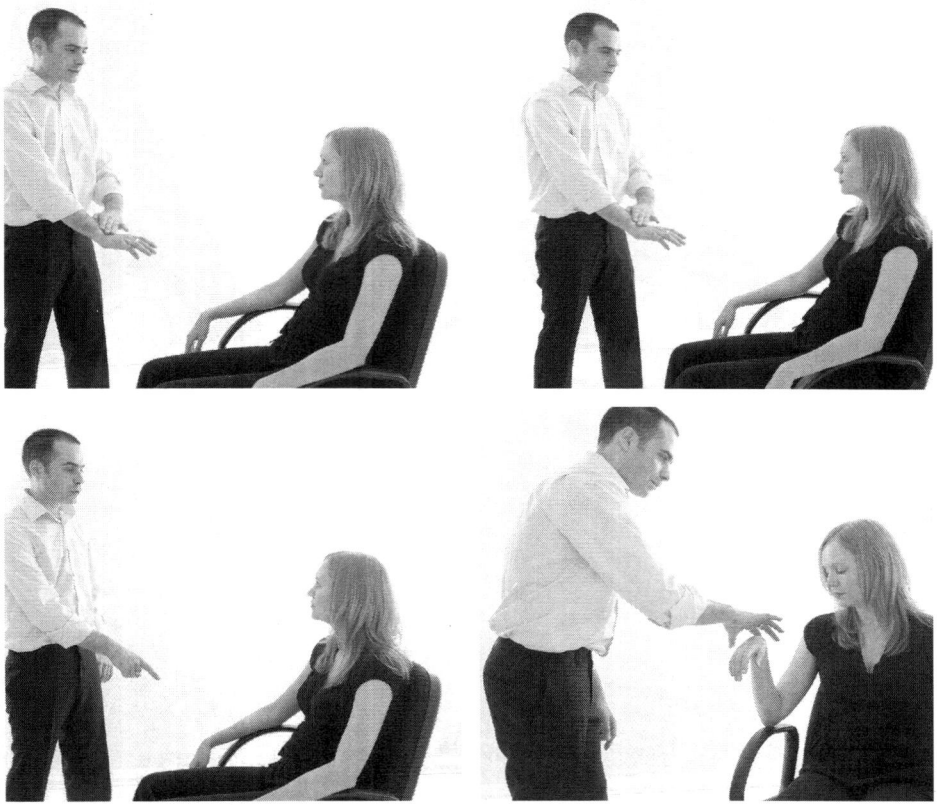

Note the permissive language 'you can allow your eyes to close'. They will close their eyes. Hold their wrist in a way that makes them wonder whether you are holding it or not and whether you are lifting it or not. A light touch sometimes lifting one of the fingers that is holding their wrist creates a kind of ambiguous touch that creates some confusion. Attempt to get to the point where their hand is 'held' just by you having one finger remaining in contact with the back of their wrist. Then re-grip and push their arm down slowly almost as if you were meeting some resistance and it was slightly difficult to push the arm down. This can be achieved by tensing the muscles in your own arm. It gives the impression to the subject that their arm is feeling slightly strange.

As you push the arm down say this.

As the arm goes down you can allow your eyes to open and relax even more.

Repeat adding some pacing comments and shifting from permissive language to a more direct command and tone. This time you are saying the 'eyes will close'.

That's right, the arm lifts and your eyes will close. I push it down and your eyes will open as you relax even more.

Pull the arm up for a third time and use the following shift in your language to suggest that the arm is lifting and the eyes are going to close automatically. Due to the built in rehearsal it probably will lift automatically.

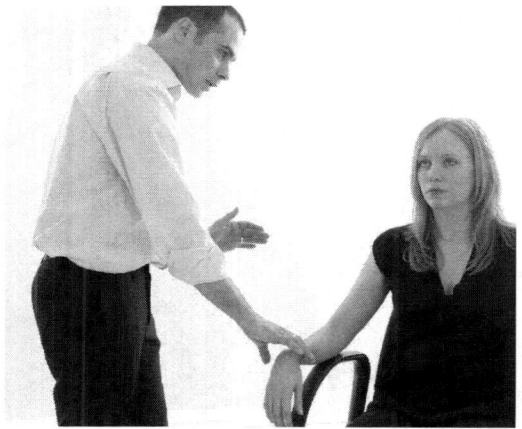

This time as the arm lifts and your eyes close, feel that wrist getting stiffer and stiffer.

As you mention their wrist squeeze it a bit to encourage tension. Poke them in the forearm muscle with the tip of your index of your second finger and say the following.

Feel that forearm muscle tightening.

Poke the elbow joint.

Feel that elbow joint stiffening.

Poke them in the bicep and shoulder as you say.

Feel that bicep stiffening…into the shoulder. Every muscle and fibre stiffer and stiffer as it hangs on that wire.

As you mention the 'wire' tap the side of your index finger on the crease of their wrist. Then continue.

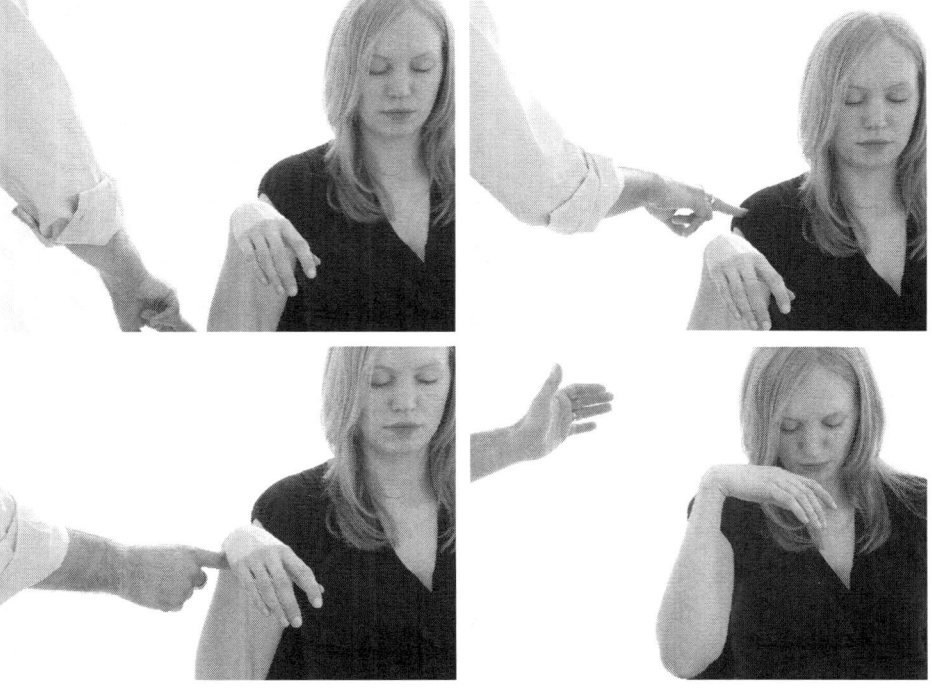

**Each word that I say and every breath that you take will take you
deeper and deeper into the trance.**

Repeat the idea that the arm is getting stiffer and intensify the trance.

You have created a situation of leverage. The subject is now in hypnosis and
in an unusual situation. Their eyes are shut and they have their arm stuck
in the air. So link the arm lifting or falling or moving toward their face to
whatever you wish.

For example the strongest next step might be to say this.

**Feel that arm getting lighter and beginning to lift up. That arm is lifting
off the chair now, getting higher and higher. Just like your head is a
magnet and your hand is a powerful magnet. When it touches your face
you will drop into a profound state of hypnosis.**

If you do not think you can encourage that hand to their face then you could
simply link it falling back to the chair to them going into a deeper state.

**In a moment I will count to three and on the number three that arm
will drift down on that imaginary wire and your eyes will remain closed
as you continue to relax and drift deeper into hypnosis. As the muscles
relax you will relax as that arm drifts down you can drift down. 1,2,3.
That's right drifting down to a comfortable resting position as you drift
deep asleep, deeper and deeper.**

4.6 Jacquin Power Induction

Not a lot to say about this other than remember at all times you are The Hypnotist. This takes confidence but even more importantly demands absolute congruence in your presentation and expectation. Rapidly establish rapport and lead your subject into complying with the set up so they are ready to be hypnotized.

OK if you could just sit back in the chair, that's right, feet on the floor and just place your hands on your lap, and relax.

Expect to see signs of hypnosis. Get their full attention. Make sure you fixate their gaze. You can do that with eye contact. Point to a spot just underneath one of your eyes and encourage them to lock onto it while you look at a single point such as one of their eyes or through their head to an imagined point at the back of the head or the bridge of their nose. If you do not wish to use your eyes then fixate their gaze on the tip of your pen or finger.

Now look at me, right here. In a moment I want you to just hear the word 'Relax' four times in your mind. The fourth time you hear that word you are going to drift into a trance and your hands will begin to lift up off of your lap. Do it now. Don't go into a deep trance until you hear that word for the fourth time.

After a few seconds continue as follows

That's right keeping your eyes open, look at me you can focus your full attention there why your unconscious mind begins to lift your hand up, I don't know if it will be a finger or a hand that moves first.

Test your work immediately by using the leverage you have gained by getting that arm up. Take it somewhere. The beautiful thing about this induction is the suggestion for hypnosis is contained within the trigger word 'Relax'. That is it, go with whatever they present you with and lead it. At any point you can command the subject's eyes to close if you prefer. If I want to do this with eyes closed I will typically link the fourth repetition of 'Relax' with the instruction to close them.
Don't close your eyes until the fourth time you hear that word 'Relax', in your mind. That's it, eyes closed now, sleep.

4.7 Instant Induction

Hold your finger or anything up in front of them and get them to focus on it. Begin moving it toward their face as you get them to take a deep breath.

Look at this, take a deep breath; now close your eyes and sleep. Deep asleep. Deeper and deeper asleep. You are going to sleep.

Like the power induction this requires absolute confidence and congruency in delivery. It can be delivered immediately following The Set Piece. The Set Piece bypasses the critical faculty and the mind is immediately encouraged to lock around the idea of sleep. Making a pass in front of their eyes or clicking your fingers will ensure their eyes close at the appropriate moment. Gently pulling the subjects head toward their chest as you say 'sleep' encourages them to go. If you get wind that someone has been hypnotized before – especially if they were part of a stage show – then you could be assured that this instant induction will work if you expect it to.

There are those that say this kind of induction is simply unrealistic and impossible unless you absolutely have a prime subject or you have already warmed them up. This all helps. This is my preferred approach when re-inducing hypnosis. The time will arise when you are standing amongst a group of people and somebody says I was hypnotized on stage once. I can't remember much about it. Great. You can have absolute confidence you will be effective.

However this kind of induction will also work with the uninitiated. Maybe not every time but if you are in the right frame of mind and they are able to be then it will more often than not work. Do not forget that the common perception of how someone is hypnotized is usually a little hazy but centres around the idea that it happens very quickly and involves commands and eyes closing. Often your subject just seems to know what to do even though they have not been there before.

Just because there is not much to an instant induction does not mean there must be much more to it. There is not – just the confidence it will work and the intention to ensure it does.

5.0 Getting Deep Now – Intensification!

Once you have induced hypnosis you can intensify the state the subject is in and make their new reality more vibrant. This process is commonly referred to as deepening. For some time I pondered whether you really have to give the subject time to get comfortable with it all - surely comfort is a subjective enough opinion. If they are 'in' surely they are 'in'. However in practice it seems to help things along if after inducing hypnosis you spend a little time ensuring they know they are doing it right, that they are safe and well and enjoying it. This gives the subject a chance to get a sense of what this new hypnotic world is like.

It gives The Hypnotist an opportunity to shore up their work so far, to give out some procedural instructions regarding 'wake up' and 'go into hypnosis' commands and to get ready to really begin directing suggestions at the unconscious. The easiest way to do this is to tell the subject to 'go deeper'.

A common view amongst many hypnotists and the public is that there are many 'levels' of hypnosis. It follows that the metaphorical associations of 'going deeper and deeper' when coupled with ambiguous ideas about 'going into' a trance result in much theorizing about how deep someone is. Strangely given all the focus on depth, many hypnotherapists continue in their work without knowing if their subject is hypnotized – the reason being that they do not test for hypnosis, light or deep, instead assuming that because their subject is looking relaxed and has their eyes closed they are hypnotized. They might be, but they might not. Rather than risk exposing this illusion they do not actually ask for a direct sign that hypnosis is established. There is no excuse for this – fear is not an excuse a hypnotist should have to use. So test your work. This is easy to do. Give the subject a suggestion and see if they respond to it – unconsciously.

It can be argued that all this discussion of levels and depth just causes confusion – there is just one level, hypnosis. It will make you more effective as The Hypnotist if you think of it this way. The subject is either hypnotized or they are not. You are either having the response to your suggestions driven by the unconscious mind, without critical inductive reasoning or you are not.

So immediately after the induction begin deepening. Recognise that by now the subject should be accepting and responding to your directions unconsciously. By all means send your subjects 'deeper and deeper and deeper'. Send them 'deep asleep', 'deep inside' and 'ten times deeper'. These words are embedded in the psyche of nearly everyone just like the word 'Sleep'. Just because you know hypnosis is not sleep and that they are not going anywhere is no reason not to use these words. In your mind be thinking about a clear line of communication with their unconscious however you perceive that. There is no need to fuss over what the subject is thinking – they have an on board model of hypnosis and whether they realise it or not they know what to do! Their unconscious automatic pattern driven abilities are becoming easier to talk to. You are no longer talking to their conscious mind. Ignore it. Your goal is to deliver a suggestion to intensify the state they believe themselves to be in.

There is no need to spend ages doing this. On stage and in the therapy room I might spend five minutes on it. In an impromptu situation it might be just a few seconds to a minute. In deepening you begin to direct your subject deeper into the state they are now in and do this in a pleasant way. There really is nothing to fight. The suggestions you are giving them are easy to follow and not objectionable in anyway.

You can continue to deepen each time you re-awaken and re-hypnotize the subject. Think of it a bit like plate spinning. Every now and again just give the subject encouragement to go deeper. If you pull this off properly then you are ready to move on from intensifying the state to directing their unconscious further and shaping their reality however you wish.

There are three main ways of deepening.

5.1 Links

A link connects one thing to another. So connect things with your directions to intensify hypnosis.

In a moment I will ask you to open your eyes and then close your eyes. When you close your eyes that is your signal to go twice as deeply relaxed/ into hypnosis. OK. Open your eyes. Now close your eyes and double that feeling, go twice as deep.

This approach is known as 'fractionation'. You go over this a few times, each time adding more suggestions. It works wonderfully. Do this and manage their gaze with yours or by holding up something for them to look at.

In a moment I will count down from 5 to 0 and with every number I go past you will double that feeling and become twice as deeply hypnotized. Picture a target in your minds eye like an archery target in the distance. As each number goes past you can drift closer to that target until it is like a giant target, so close you can pass right through the middle of it. On the other side of that bulls-eye is a profound state of hypnosis, you will enjoy. Now, start drifting 5, closer and closer, 4 deeper and deeper, 3 just the sound of my voice as you drift, 2 deeper and deeper, looking forward to drifting through that bulls-eye, 1....zero. All the way through, you are going to sleep.

You could ditch the visualisation of a target and simply count down and associate going deeper with each number. You can encourage the subject to repeat in their mind as they go past each number 'I am becoming more deeply hypnotised' or 'I am doubling my state of relaxation'. Other visual metaphors could be walking down a flight of steps or going down in a lift then stepping through the door into a profound state of hypnosis. Personally I am not a fan of those but they seem to work just fine. There is no need to go out on a huge rambling description of a magic garden then a beach and then some steps. You might end up below sea level! Keep it short and peppered with suggestions that will turn things up a level. Another simple link is to associate going back into hypnosis with going twice as deep as before.

Each time I say the word sleep you will return into this state of hypnosis going twice as deep as before.

Here is another example.

In a moment I am going to touch the back of your hand and it will begin to lift up toward your face. As it (touch hand) begins to feel lighter and lighter and lift up all by itself you can enjoy a wonderful sense of well being, as you continue to drift deeper into hypnosis. The closer it gets to your face the more relaxed you become.

This is a little bolder because you about to test your work so far by giving them a suggestion that you are expecting them to act on. When their hand lifts associate it with going deeper. Give it a physical target or point in space to aim at – like their head or face - this builds some expectation that when it gets there they will go even deeper still. Indeed when using any technique with some movement or repetitive behaviour associate the process and completion of the process to something you want the subject to do or feel. In this case that would be depth.

5.2 Loops

These statements create a feedback loop that will intensify hypnosis. They create associations that feed off of each other. Some are short-lived loops and some are continuous.

Go deeper as you notice your eyes flickering, as you drift deeper and deeper they will flicker even more.

The deeper you go the better you feel and the better you feel the deeper you go.

Even as you wonder how deeply you have drifted, you can continue to drift down deeper relaxed.

As your body moves and relaxes (With one hand on the subjects shoulder rock their body gently back and forward encouraging muscle relaxation) **go deeper and deeper as it relaxes even more. That's right, your legs will support you even as you continue relaxing, deeper and deeper.**

5.3 Chains

Every breath you take will send you deeper and deeper.

Every word I say will send you deeper and deeper.

Every beat of your heart will take you deeper and deeper to sleep.

Every number I go past, every breath you take and every beat of your heart is doubling the relaxation.

I am sure you get the idea. If you can associate something in ongoing experience that is not going to stop then you have a chain – a step up from a link. This is also a good time to begin giving some directions that makes clear what you expect of them.

6.0 Direction

Words are your major means of giving suggestions, ideas or what I prefer to call directions to your subject. It is also possible to use actions, sounds and by merely hinting at what you want. You want the subjects mind to lock around the ideas you give it. Therefore it is important to deliver all of your suggestions with clarity, complete confidence and absolute assurance and to do so in a positive manner.

Speak clearly with command and authority without being abrasive or inattentive. You can usher their mind gently in a given direction and also radically shunt it where you want it. Use your vocal tone to describe your ideas, excite their unconscious mind. Rambling in a low gravely tone is not necessary. Be yourself, just a little more animated as if you were talking to a smart child about an exciting thing they are going to do or somewhere they are going to go. Be descriptive but not too detailed. Let their mind fill in the blanks.

It is preferable that the directions you give do not bring the subjects critical faculties into action. If you have said 'you are on a beach' and then followed it later with 'look at the pebbly beach' it might jar them because they are on a white sandy beach. So if you want them on a pebbly beach put them on one from the start. Your aim is to put a couple of brush strokes on their mental canvas and allow them to generate a reality from that.

Rather than challenging it and negotiating with their conscious mind it is far easier to walk around it. Give suggestions that make your other suggestions easy to accept.

For example if I wanted to steal an expensive watch off of the wrist of my subject it would be possible to do that by just asking him to give me the watch. It is much easier though to tell them that the watch belongs to me, or at least that their arm is completely numb then remove it.

If I walked up to a policeman and asked him to drive me around town in his car he would likely judge that to be an unrealistic request and one he could not act on. If he was hypnotized to believe I was his Chief Superintendent or The Prime Minister it would be quite a reasonable request that he could act upon immediately.

Try to avoid colloquialisms of language or things that are so dated or of uncommon knowledge that they might not be understood or could be misinterpreted. In one performance of mine I was assembling a line of subjects who on command would do some kind of bizarre movement or exercise that would trigger the next in line to do theirs. The first did star jumps, another sit ups, another a moon walk. One of the row was instructed that she would 'do the electric boogaloo, that her arms would do the greatest electric wave' – in my mind I was imagining a break-dancer, but her unconscious, a little younger than mine, had not heard of the electric wave – so she started rolling about all over the floor with her arms waving about like Kate Bush, I assume believing she was a wave of some kind. Just because you put the direction in does not mean you know exactly where it is going to take the subject. That is half the fun of hypnosis and a good reason to give the subject your full attention.

Make your directions a statement of fact. If you want someone to bite into an onion believing it is a peach, do not ask them to imagine it is a peach. Tell them you are going to hand them a peach. If you want them to believe you are Denzel Washington, do not ask them to imagine that, tell them they will believe you are the global movie star Denzel Washington.

You are changing their beliefs therefore their reality – not just asking them to imagine.

6.1 The Super Suggestion

As a child were you ever asked if you found a magical lamp and a genie popped out and granted you one wish, what would it be?

Did you ever wish for more wishes?

As The Hypnotist you want your subject to accept your suggestions. By the time you have done your Set Piece, your induction and deepening they have already accepted plenty so it follows that giving them a suggestion that they will accept all of your suggestions from this point until you say otherwise is a smart move. Give them the wonderful direction that they will follow all of your directions. This is what some call the Super Suggestion (15).

A particular attitude must be adopted to deliver these words effectively. They are that strong. This is not the place for doubts. If you have any keep them to yourself or better still flush them out and get rid of them.

From this moment, everything I say now is your reality, every single thing. You know what I say you know, you will do what I ask you to do, feel what I say you can feel and see what I say you can see. Everything I say is instantly your reality without doubt, question or hesitation because you have a super powerful mind. You will follow perfectly every direction I give you.

Immediately prove this fact to yourself and the subject. Test them. Give them a suggestion that requires a direct hypnotic response and see if they follow it. You could do a stiff arm or hand levitation. You could 'magnetise' or 'glue' their hand to something. I prefer to make the subjects hand and head magnetic and encourage an irresistible pull between them, when they touch stick them together. This is not asking as much of the subject as positive visual hallucinations but is still entirely convincing to them. You are ratifying the fact that the Super Suggestion has landed. From this point on it should be plain sailing.

The words above are just a suggestion. You can find your own just so long as they communicate clearly that all of your suggestions will be accepted.

6.2 Encouragement

Let your subject know how brilliant they are and how well they are doing. Do this before, during and after your time with them. Everyone likes to know that they are doing well. If they believe they are a good subject and you hold that belief they will be.

The stage hypnotist's subjects have the laughter and applause of the audience to encourage them. Working one to one you can and should make up for that. Encouraging remarks, gestures and contact do so much.

- It lets the subject know that they are doing things correctly.
- It gives a gentle nod to the conscious mind that all is well.
- It ratifies and reinforces what they have achieved so far.
- It keeps the mood light and creative.
- It suggests that you are on the same side as your subject.

You have a natural ability to go into hypnosis / you have a super powerful mind / you are doing brilliantly.

You have a conscious mind and a super powerful unconscious mind. A wonderful resource you can learn from.

That's right.

Great job. You are an absolute star.

You're doing brilliantly.

If you have an audience let them know that when you wake the subject up you want them to show their appreciation with a massive round of applause. Let the subject know that this will make them feel good.

6.3 Procedural Instructions

Once you have done your deepening it is useful to give some procedural instructions. To begin with make clear that whenever you say 'Sleep' they will immediately return to the state of hypnosis going even deeper than before. When you say '1, 2 wide awake' they will open their eyes and be able to move and speak and act on the suggestions you have given them. Ask them to nod their head if they understand. You can of course substitute these words for your own – just be consistent.

From this moment when I touch you on the shoulder and say 'Sleep' you will immediately return to this state of hypnosis going deeper each time. When I touch you on the shoulder and say 'Eyes open, wide awake' you will be able to move and speak normally in every way but act on the suggestions I have given to you. Nod your head if you understand.

Consider health and safety and give suggestions accordingly. Then tell them that if for any reason they had to return to full alertness or leave the building in a hurry that they would do so and feel great, completely free of any suggestion that had been given to them.

Sometimes the subject will experience complete amnesia for the suggestions they have been given. However amnesia is not guaranteed, so if you want amnesia for the suggestion you have given them insist upon it. Tell them that when you say 1, 2 wide awake they will have complete amnesia for the suggestion you have given them but will act on it anyway. This permits some wonderful mind reading routines. Use your imagination.

Really get this part of your approach mastered so that you can fire through it quickly. It all helps by letting them know who is in control, it communicates to them and other observers that you care and they are in safe hands and generally keeps the whole thing flowing more easily making it much simpler to keep them in the state you want them to be in.

6.4 Navigation Control

Once you have got to the point where you have satisfied yourself that your subject is hypnotized and given and tested the super suggestion and issued the procedural instructions that will help things along it is time to begin really directing the subject to do whatever it is you want them to.

It is worth having a plan. Establish at least two or three routines – that are appropriate for any place or environment that you are an expert in. Most hypnotists have some 'pet' routines that they use to get things moving.

Keep it simple see how they respond and then encourage more.

I tend to start small and build into bigger responses throughout each routine. There is no real reason for this, as by this point the subject should be pretty 'plastic'. However it provides some structure to what I am doing and if there is any truth in the idea that the subject is well served by getting into their hypnotic world gradually it takes care of that too. Typically I begin by getting some emotional and physical responses from the subject. Things such as arm levitation, catalepsy, sticking them to something work well. Typical emotional changes that can be linked to these physical responses such as making them laugh or bliss out are easy to invoke. Often I will follow this with my amnesia routine, then something that requires the subject to show off their verbal skills and then hallucinations of some kind. The routines outlined for applying hypnosis in section 7.0 will make this clear.

Some of the best ideas develop out of impromptu moments and the unexpected response of your subject. So give them time to respond and remember that while they are responding to one suggestion they are still going to respond to more. They will say what you tell them to say. So help them along giving their receptive unconscious an absolutely clear idea of what you want from it.

Following any major course of directions should you want to set off down a different path the easiest thing to do is to simply command them back to sleep. They are essentially back in neutral then. It makes for a cleaner run into the next direction you take them. Sometimes you get a slightly confused attitude from the subject if you just keep stacking more and more on top of them without first getting rid of some of the old stuff. My experience is that in practice you do not always have to undo what you just did but in practice it is a useful rule of thumb to do so. So undo the last suggestion then give a fresh one. It makes it easier for The Hypnotist too.

7.0 Applying Impromptu Hypnosis

Rather than provide a long list of hundreds of possible routines or ideas about what to do with your hypnotized subject, I have written up in detail some routines that I have done in an impromptu setting.

Some of these are things I do regularly in impromptu demonstrations, the therapy room, and training. Some are typical 'stage' routines done off stage and finally some are odd impromptu one off things that I hope will get your creative mind going about what you can achieve using impromptu hypnosis. I encourage you to use your imagination in coming up with routine ideas. If almost anything is possible, and it is with hypnosis, what would you want them to do? Use your imagination and let your subject use theirs.

I have included everything from the initial Set Up, The Set Piece, the Induction, Intensification, Super Suggestion, testing and direction. Although some of the routines outlined here involve 'borrowing' property or getting free goods, I do not suggest that this is ethical or what you should be doing. It is just part of my performance. I almost always give the subject back their stuff, unless of course it is something I really want. I am kidding of course. All of these routines have been done for real in impromptu settings and are here to simply give you ideas about what is possible. Nothing has been added or taken away.

7.1 Briefest Therapy – The Hypnotic Corpse

This is a routine I have used hundreds of times. It makes the subject laugh with abandon and allows the hypnotist to cue that laughter on command. You are essentially going to link the automatic lifting of an arm and its proximity to the face as a sliding gauge of mirth.

I often do this after a session of hypnotherapy when I teach my client how they can do instant self hypnosis. However I have also done it mid session and as an impromptu piece in many different settings. On stage this is often the first routine I get into after giving everyone on stage a stiff arm. In an impromptu demonstration it is often the first real bit of suggestion I go for after the induction. My wording rarely strays far from what follows. I use it with groups as well as one to one. I have had feedback that this was worth the entire cost of a hypnotherapy session - as the subject had clearly and unexpectedly shifted some huge emotional hang up with it - even though it was really just being said by me as a convincer to the subject that she had of course been hypnotized. On a lighter note once you have set this up it means you can cue someone to laugh with complete abandon on command, which is quite entertaining. Just tell them not to think about that thing.

The first step in the routine is to get their hand moving toward their face 'all by itself'. I will assume you have already done some hypnosis with them, given them a trigger to go back into hypnosis and had some physical phenomena such as arm levitation. This is the ideal place to begin. However it is not too tough to get a hand moving toward a face from cold so if you have to work a little harder to get to that point so be it – you could do this as a Set Piece or from any of the inductions that result in a hand being in front of the face. Of course once you have the arm lifting it is the same spiel from there on in.

There is obvious opportunity for tonal emphasis on phrases like 'feel differently' 'smile' 'laugh'. I have phrased the script to give a gradual build so by the time I am saying 'laugh' and 'funny' I should have already got a smile out of them. Timing and pacing is quite crucial - so as ever say what you see and then lead a little, say it with a smile on your face. Try and time the 'burst out laughing' to the moment the hand touches the face. They normally continue corpsing with the tiniest little bit of plate spinning from you, giving an opportunity to do some general feel good work. If someone is in pain, they will be laughing their aches and pains away, if in fear, laughing those doubts and fears away - but that is all extra. Just get them corpsing. If other people around are laughing, and you will find unbridled hypnotic laughter is contagious, then utilise that too.

When you have been hypnotized like that it is easy for you to go back into a trance instantly and immediately at your own command. You might wonder why you would like to do that. Well firstly it is a fantastic tool, a way of deeply relaxing. As well as this it can be used to direct your unconscious resources toward those things you wish to achieve. If you are happy to I'll show you how to do it.

Get agreement from them.

OK, again just place your feet flat on the floor and your hands lightly on your lap (arm of the chair). **I'd like you to just look at the back of your hand and pick one spot, like a hair or a line or something. Now don't close your eyes yet, just focus on that point and when you are ready I would like you to hear the word relax four times in your mind and the fourth time your hear it, just allow your eyes to close, that's right do it now, and as your eyes close you will immediately drift back into that trance state. This time I'd like you to pay attention to the small changes that occur, some barely noticeable, in the relaxation of your face, your breathing has shifted slightly, quite at ease.**

And in a moment that hand is going to start drifting up toward your face all by itself. That's right; you might notice those sensations increasing, fingers twitching and just like those hands were magnets you will feel that inevitable pull between your hand and your face.

As it lifts you will enjoy a growing sense of well being, the closer it gets to your face the better you are going to feel and the better you feel the lighter it will get. That's it, lighter and lighter.

Now I came across this funny idea that there is something you would love to feel differently about, something that if you could smile about it, if you could laugh about it, you would be so much better off. And as that hand gets closer to your face for some unknown reason it is going to start to seem funny to you, that's right, for some unknown reason, and as that smile begins to grow, that's it, it is going to turn into a giggle and the closer it gets the funnier it seems, funnier and funnier, the closer it

gets the less serious you become, and when that hand touches your face you are going to burst out laughing and never again will you feel the way you used to, it will be all you can do to try to stop yourself laughing as inappropriately as possible, even when you think about it now it seems hilarious to you.

Now every time I click my fingers it will seem 10 times funnier. Like the funniest scene from the funniest film you can remember only now it is 100 times funnier.

By this point if there are no tears of laughter running down their cheeks or snot running down their face I would be disappointed.

Now in a moment that arm will begin drifting down to your lap again only as quickly as you can drift down into an even deeper state of hypnosis, a state of absolute bliss. Sleep.

Bring them out.

Eyes open wide awake.

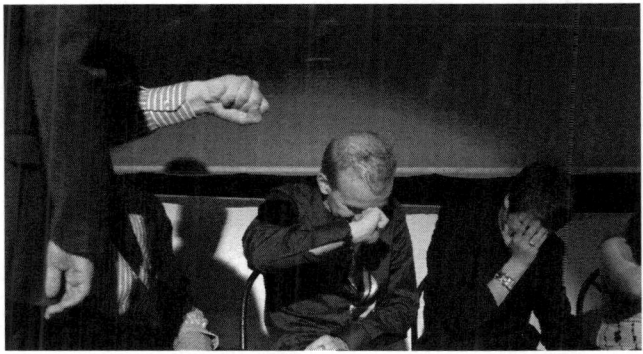

Brilliant, how good did that feel. Now this was something you used to take seriously was it not? (Cue laughter).

When you have a hand in the air it is another opportunity to give it something to do. For example once the subjects hand is touching their forehead give the suggestion,

Get ready to Sleep deeply now... and when I say three your hand will fall down to your lap and you will be fast asleep, 1, 2, 3. Sleep.

7.2 Rossi Style Brief Therapy

This is a very simple exercise inspired by Ernest Rossi's seminal work (16). I have added more suggestion to it and instead of just using it as intended, as a diagnostic tool, try to squeeze quite a lot more use out of it. Do not be fooled by its simplicity. I use it as The Set Piece, as an induction, as a genuine vehicle for content free therapy, as well as a diagnostic and therapeutic tool. In the example below I am aiming it at an unspecified problem 'x'.

Please put both hands out in front of you and focus your attention on the space between them.

Now close your eyes and picture those hands out in front of you.

That's right and focus on that image in your mind as you feel the magnetic force develop between those hands, in your mind you can imagine that force beginning to pull those hands together.

Now, only as quickly as your unconscious mind is ready to deal with this problem (assimilate learning's, show you how powerful it is; take you into hypnosis) **therapeutically today I would like those hands to be pulled together.**

Like two magnets moving closer and closer, that's right and the closer they get the stronger that force becomes. That's right you can notice that movement. You can try and hold them steady and find you cannot and when those fingers touch your arms will stay out there while you can just relax.

Now I would like one of those hands to drift down only as quickly as your unconscious mind can review all of the memories and experiences associated with this (problem) only when it has fully reviewed that will your hand will drift down to your lap. That's it in its own time. All the way down.

The hand should drift down cataleptically.

Now I would like the unconscious to move that other hand down towards your lap only as quickly as your unconscious mind can identify all of the resources required to put this (problem) behind you today and forever. All the learning's and the resources required, putting this behind you forever. That hand will drift down and touch your lap only as quickly as you have identified all of the resources and made the changes necessary to put this behind you forever.

Will your unconscious mind nod your head to let me know these changes have been made?

You can then just proceed with a deepening of the trance, go immediately into another technique or alternatively just ask them to open their eyes – in other words leave them in trance. It can be useful to do this prior to the 'real' work, do it as a Set Piece. They can listen and talk to you. A great way to leave someone in hypnosis is to tell them that when you count from 1 to 3 they will be wide awake and normal in every way. Then after a few other comments say '1, 2 eyes open'. They may even wonder if they are in a trance, you do not need to mention trance or hypnosis.

I suggest you do this early after questions then proceed as normal with a discussion. It will make it easier to read their unconscious communication and also make your efforts to embed suggestions prior to trance more successful.

Of course this procedure has three steps - hands together, one arm down and other arm down. In the example given those three steps are for a particular purpose – to deal with a problem. You can change any or all of the steps. For example link the hands together to the mind signalling it's readiness for you to be hypnotized, one hand down for the body to relax and the other hand down for the mind to relax.

7.3 Gone!

The first time you make yourself invisible using your hypnotic powers is likely to be a bit of an event. It certainly was for me anyway. It can, unless you suggest otherwise, freak the subject out a bit, especially if you start moving things around the room such as lifting up chairs, pouring cups of water, throwing things at them or scaring them with a puppet. When you realise they cannot see you it might freak you a bit too, so hold yourself together. If you do not want them knocked too far sideways understand that you can direct how they feel so tell them that they will find it incredible but will not be afraid. Or tell them they will be afraid, very afraid but will not leave the room or their chair. The choice is yours.

OK can I try something with you? Great. Can you make yourself comfortable, feet on the floor, hands resting on your lap. Now look at me, right here.

Point to just underneath your right eye and look into one of the subject's eyes.

In a moment you are going to go into a trance. I don't want you to close your eyes yet, just keep looking at that spot, now when you are ready repeat the word 'Relax' four times in your mind. The fourth time you repeat that word you can allow your eyes to close and you will immediately begin drifting to sleep, deep asleep, deeply into a trance. You will know you are in it because one of those hands is going to begin lifting up toward your face, that's it. Lighter and lighter just like your head is a magnet and your hand is a magnet – tune into that real or imagined magnetic force developing between your head and that hand and the closer it gets the deeper you will go. The deeper you go the better you feel. When that hand touches your face you will double the physical and mental relaxation.

Now in a moment I am going to click my fingers and that hand will drop down into your lap like a wet rag. When it touches your lap that is your signal to go even deeper into a profound state of hypnosis.

(Click)

Deeper and deeper. Everything I say now will become your reality.

Every single thing, without doubt, question or hesitation will become your reality. You know what I say you know, see what I say you can see and feel what I say you feel. Everything I say is instantly your reality.

Next prove that the super suggestion has landed by giving a relatively simple idea to latch onto. Normally I go into the Stiff Arm exercise using it as a routine rather than a Set Piece.

In a moment I am going to borrow your arm. That's right, now make a tight fist. That's right and as you feel that tight fist, that arm is going to become stiffer and stiffer, every muscle nerve and fibre, stiffer and stiffer, there is a steel bar running from your shoulder down through your arm all the way to that fist, you cannot bend it no matter how hard you try. Try and bend it and find you cannot. You are a strong man, try and bend it and find it gets stiffer and stiffer. That's it as it begins to shake it gets stiffer still.

Push their arm down as you belt out this command.

Now sleep!

In a moment I am going to click my fingers your eyes will open and you will look up, you will no longer be able to see me or anything I am wearing, everything else will be normal but you will no longer be able to see me or anything I am wearing. You will be able to hear me and feel my touch but you will no longer be able to see me.

The subject will normally just wake up and look forward like nothing is out of the ordinary because it isn't yet – they just cannot see you. So when you move if you look at them you will notice that they do not give you any attention. Their gaze is not automatically drawn to your movement. Pour a glass of water or wave things in front of the subject – like a set of keys. Throw a chair in the air and catch it. Speak to them.

Sleep! When I click my fingers your eyes will open and everything will be back to normal in every way, you will be able to see me.

Alternatively say they will be able to see your body but not your head!

7.4 Robbed!

In this example I hypnotized a market stall holder at his stall on a busy Friday lunchtime. I gave him a post hypnotic suggestion that when I tapped him on the shoulder he would immediately return to sleep and that the next time he saw me he would have no conscious recollection of meeting me before or anything I have said. I awoke him and left. I returned an hour later and went through a three stage 'stage' hypnosis routine built around a cucumber (18).

My intention was to get him to give me some of his produce for free. I left with a bin liner full of cucumbers. In this example I used each phase of The Set Piece as a hypnotic induction but did not test it, just observed and then did the Handshake Induction.

Hi so are you up for this? Let's see if you can be hypnotized. We are going to start with a couple of simple exercises to fire up your concentration and imagination. I am going to give you some simple instructions and I want you to follow these instructions. If I ask you in imagine something I want you to do your best to, if I ask you to use your gut feeling then do so. Nod your head if you understand. Great.

So please put your hands out in front of you.

I then proceeded with the Magnetic Fingers as an induction. As soon as the fingers touched I said the following.

Now close your eyes and sleep, deep asleep. As I rock your body back and forward just go in deep, deep asleep. Notice how good it feels to relax like that because in a moment I am going to show you how to go even deeper. When I touch you on the shoulder and say eyes open wide awake your eyes will open and you will look at me. When I say sleep you will return to this state going even deeper than before. Nod your head if you understand.

I then immediately got into Magnetic Hands. When the hands touched I went into induction mode again pushing the subjects head forward as I said 'Sleep' and immediately intensified things, building in everything I had learnt about the subject from the first phase. I then woke him again and went into a handshake induction immediately afterwards and this time emphasised sleep and deepened the state even more. I gave the super suggestion and then a post hypnotic trigger for hypnosis and amnesia for meeting me.

When I return you will have no idea who I am. It will feel like we have never met before. When I touch you on the shoulder and say sleep you will immediately return to this state, instantly and immediately going even deeper than before.

When I returned an hour later I walked up to the market stall and grabbed a cucumber. I held this up high and pointed at the end of it and asked the subject

How much are these?

His attention now arrested and mind confused I continued.

How much? Have a look at it, here right at the end of it, come a bit closer, because now an interesting thing is going to happen, let me show you something as you look at it.

I leant forward and tapped him on the shoulder as I gave him the post hypnotic suggestion to go back into hypnosis.

Sleep, now all the way in, go deeper, deeper, deeper down. That arm can relax, completely relax, that arm can relax completely relax you are going to sleep. Every breath you take and every word I say now will take you deeper and deeper into that state. You are drifting to sleep. Your head can fall forward onto your chest as you go deeper and deeper to sleep. Everything I say now, every single thing I say will instantly become your reality, without doubt or question. You see what I say you can see, know what I say you know and do what I say you will do. Everything I say is your reality.

You are the world's greatest cigar connoisseur. You love fine cigars and I am going to hand you the world's finest cigar to smoke. Eyes open, wide awake. Here you go, have a go on that. You can bite the end off of it first.

He bit the end off right through the plastic covering and I offered him a light. I encouraged him to comment on the cigars qualities, its strength and taste, while he had a few puffs.

Sleep and stand. Deep asleep. All the way in. Deep asleep. Your legs will support you as you go deeper to sleep. The next time you open your eyes you will realise you are holding the world's biggest spliff. It is the world's strongest joint. The strongest marijuana and you are going to enjoy smoking it. Eyes open wide awake.

Have a go on that. Have another all the way down to your toes this time.

Again I encouraged him to savour the flavour and strength.

Sleep and stand. When you I click my fingers you will open your eyes and realise the drugs squad are about to raid this stall. All of those cucumbers are incredibly strong spliffs. You are going to put them in a bag and urgently insist I take them away from this stall. I will resist but you will insist. Eyes open wide awake.

Look. Filth (Police). **Have you got a bag?**

He hastily grabbed a bin liner and proceeded to fill it with cucumbers.

I repeatedly insisted 'I can't take them all'. He of course insisted that I could.

Quick, load them all in there. That's it. Stash the rest, stash them.

I walked off with a bin liner full of cucumbers.

As this was an experimental one off I later returned his produce. I thought it would be useful to go through the exact wake up procedure used. If I do stuff like this for entertainment purposes I always return and hypnotise the subject again and do a proper wake up procedure. Ten minutes later he was still in somewhat of a shifty panic to see me returning with the 'drugs' and asked me what I was doing as he glanced about for the police. I simply thanked him and did a handshake induction on him and proceeded to first deepen the experience, do some feel good work and fully reawaken him 'back in the market' everything back to normal.

Hello, thanks for...

Extended hand for handshake and went into handshake induction and immediate deepening of the hypnotic state.

Look at your hand…now sleep.

The wake up procedure followed.

In a moment I will count up to five and on the count of five you will be back completely wide awake and normal able to move speak and think freely and normally. All of the things I have suggested to you up here will be gone and everything will be back to normal in every way. You will open your eyes and stretch and you will feel fantastic and ready for a wonderful afternoon of business in the market. You will feel refreshed and revitalised as if you have woken up from a wonderful night of sleep, but understand hypnosis is not sleep and the next time you get in bed to sleep you will sleep wonderfully and awake at an appropriate time refreshed and revitalised. So get ready.

One.
More aware of your body now. Every muscle, nerve and fibre coming alive.
Two.
Feel a surge of energy whizzing in through your fingers and toes into your arms, legs, up your spine, and neck to the top of your head.
Three. Take a deep breath in of cool clear air sending a surge of oxygen through your body and brain.
Four.
Your head is washed through with cool, clear water, the back of your eyes clear, nose clear, throat clear, chest and stomach clear.
Five.
Eyes open and wide awake, stretch.

Deliver this wake up call with the same amount of importance and purpose as any other directions, or preferably even more. Just because you will use your wake up over and over there is no reason for it to become dry because of a lack of delivery. At this point the subject is still hypnotized and receiving suggestions. So keep it simple and make it count. Welcome your subjects back with a big smile. Then distract them.

Thanks. Feeling good? Is there an electrical stall near here?

7.5 Cloaked!

My aim was to steal a coat from someone. I have used this approach outlined here numerous times. It illustrates how you can create a context for hypnosis and how this approach bypasses the will.

Pacing around Leicester Square I spotted someone holding a huge 'Pizza Hut This Way' sign. I asked him how long he had to stand there and the poor lad said 8 hours. I let him know I was a hypnotist and could give him time distortion. I asked him if I could make the eight hours whizz by like one hour would that be good. He agreed it would. To get started I told him to stare at the screw that attached his sign to the pole and did an eye fixation induction. I proved it was working by telling him his hands were going to lift up toward his face. I encouraged him to try and resist. Then gave the suggestions. Firstly the Super Suggestion, then a lengthy ramble about time distortion. Finally I suggested that when he opened his eyes he would realise he had my coat on and would give it back to me. He came to, I asked for my coat and he emptied his pockets and gave it to me.

Hi. Do you mind me asking how long have you got to stand here for? Eight hours! Wow. I am a hypnotist. If I could make that time whizz by and feel like just one hour how good would that feel? Are you up for being hypnotized? I am not going to make you do anything stupid and guarantee this will seem like the shortest night of your working life. Great. Well using hypnosis it is very common for people to experience time distortion. A bit like when we doze off and it only feels like we have been sleeping for a few moments but in fact it is an hour. So I want to show you how you can recreate that feeling. First of all please understand that hypnosis is not sleep and in a moment when I say sleep you will understand it is not like the sleep you have when you get in bed it is just a deep relaxation of your nervous system. You will still be able to hear me and respond when I ask you to. Now what I would like you to do is just look at this screw right in front of you. I will hold the pole.

Now look at it, do not look at me or anywhere else. You do not have to say anything or do anything. Just keep your eyes fixed on that point. As it moves closer to your face you can notice the changing focus of your eyes and when you are ready to be hypnotized close your eyes, that's right, eyes closing now, and with your eyes closed all that is important is the sound of my voice and your thoughts, that drift through your mind, no

outside sound is important to you now, just my voice. With every breath you take and every word I say now you will drift deeper and deeper into hypnosis. Your legs will support you as you go deep asleep, as I rock your shoulder letting every muscle relax now going deep asleep, completely relaxed. In a moment one of your arms is going to begin lifting upwards toward the sky, it will begin to feel lighter and lighter and lift up. As it lifts up all by itself you can try and keep it steady and find it just wants to lift right up, lighter and lighter, there it goes, up, up pulled up by an invisible force. You are doing brilliantly. When I touch that arm it will drop back down to your side and you will go even deeper into that state of hypnosis ready to really listen. From this moment when I say the word sleep you will instantly and immediately return to this state of hypnosis going even deeper than before, when I say eyes open, wide awake you will open your eyes and be able to speak and move normally in every way, you will act upon everything I say instantly and immediately, without doubt or question, fully awake and alert. When you leave work you will reflect on time having flown by really quickly as if you had simply been thinking about something else entirely. Because you know, standing there, time changes too, just like other times you may have stood in a queue and every second seems like a minute and other times on a return journey from somewhere time just flying by in a flash, and a long time feels like no time at all.

In a moment I am going to wake you up and you will be feeling fantastic, you will realise that you are wearing my coat, you are wearing my coat. You will remove it and give it back to me and be glad to do so.

Eyes open wide awake. Great. Feeling good?

I handed the subject the pole.

Shall I take it off of you?

I took back the pole to prompt him to remove his coat. He began to empty his pockets. I continued to keep him mildly confused with some random comments and questions.

Sorry is it this way round? That could confuse you.
Which way is it to Pizza Hut? OK. I will get you a fresh one.

I exchanged the pole for the coat. I walked off in the opposite direction.

7.6 Fed!

I approached Tommy – a barrow boy from one of London's East End markets. He told me that he had been hypnotized by his Sergeant-Major during his time in the army 45 years ago.

So suspecting he might be used to being ordered into hypnosis I first of all flattered him telling him that anyone who has been hypnotized has a natural ability to tap into their mind and that this ability never leaves you. I adopted quite an authoritarian approach going straight into magnetic palms as an induction. I re-orientated him and did a stiff arm, then slammed that arm down and commanded sleep. I gave him a post hypnotic suggestion for returning to hypnosis and amnesia for meeting me. Following that I left the stall and returned 30 minutes later.

Hi. I would like three pounds of apples. Three pounds of pears please. Oh and four cauliflowers. How much?

He answered 8 pounds.

Sleep.

In a moment your arm will begin lifting up above your head just like it is being pulled up on a winch. There it goes, you may be aware that it is moving but there is nothing you can do except go deeper and deeper into hypnosis now. As it lifts with every breath you take and every word I say now go deeper and deeper.

At this point I gave him the super suggestion followed by the following set of directions.

In a moment I will wake you up and you will believe that everything I place into your hand is money. Anything paper is a note, anything else is a coin. You will gratefully accept my payment and get on with your day in the normal way feeling great.

Eyes open wide wake.

Sorry, how much?

Eight pounds, here is five.

I placed a serviette in his hand followed by three bottle tops.

That is 6, 7 and 8. Is that right?

Great. Bye.

7.7 Watered!

Anyone can get free drinks. It is possible for any of us to cajole, to beg or perhaps blag someone into buying a drink. It is much much easier if the barman believes you are his favourite movie star. Buzzing from a prior hypno attack on a coffee shop and several free espressos, on the last sunny Friday of the summer, I went into a large busy bar in Soho, London. As one of the barman walked past collecting glasses I stopped and asked him who his favourite movie star was. He looked confused and said he did not know. I persisted.

'Well there must be one that you rate, a film star whose movies you like'?

He said 'Denzel'. I thanked him and off he went, he continued doing his work. At this point I had not introduced myself as a hypnotist, in fact I had not introduced myself at all. I left and then 10 minutes later came back in and walked straight up to the bar mentally primed with the intention to become Denzel.

As I stepped up to take a seat on one of the bar stools I stuck out my hand to shake hands with the Barman I had met minutes earlier.

Hi what's your name?

I grabbed his hand as he replied 'Jo', I lifted it and showed him the palm of his hand.

Look at that hand Jo, look at one spot on it, look at that spot on your hand as it moves closer to your face notice the changing focus of your eyes now close your eyes. Sleep. Go deep asleep. Just relax your arms.

I moved his other arm off of the bar so it could hang by his side.

Relax every muscle, every nerve, every fibre, you are drifting to sleep.

At this point I put my hand behind his neck and applied slight pressure encouraging his head to drop forward as I continued to give him instructions.

Your head can fall forward like a bowling ball as you relax and go deep asleep now, deep asleep, deep, deep, deep, deep asleep.

His spine started to relax allowing his head to drop forward, the bar was a little sticky so I placed my hand on the bar as a landing mat for his forehead.

Your head will rest on my hand, you are safe you are well and protected as you go deep asleep. As I rock your shoulders you can go 10 times deeper. Every breath you take and every word I say sends you deeper and deeper into that sleep. That's it, everything I say now is your reality, without doubt or question, every single thing I say will instantly become your reality however stupid or silly it seems, you know what I say you know, see what I say you see and believe I am who I say I am, everything I say is your reality. Nod your head if you understand. In a moment your left arm is going to begin drifting up toward the ceiling, it will lift up all by itself and there is nothing you can do about it. As it lifts you will go even deeper into that state of hypnosis, even more deeply relaxed. That's right it is starting to go, fingers twitching, hand moving, elbow bending, lighter and lighter as it is pulled up, you can try and keep it steady and find you cannot, it just lifts up, up, up, try and hold it down and find it lifts even higher. When I snap my fingers your hand will drop down like a wet dish cloth and you will drop down with it deeper asleep (click). I am going to count 1, 2, 3 and your eyes will open and you will stand up and you will believe I am Denzel Washington, the world famous movie star Denzel Washington. You will simply want to serve me exactly what I ask for, on the house, nothing will give you or your manager more pleasure. 1, 2, 3 wide awake. Hi I am Denzel. I'd like four drinks; I am here with a few friends of mine. Can I come behind the bar? That's how we do it in the States.

I went behind the bar and chose my drinks. I considered but then dismissed the idea of telling him I was the Manager and needed him to give me all of the notes out of the till except for the five pound notes. After getting my drinks I thanked him and got him to advertise his new reality.

Thanks it has been fantastic to meet you, you are an absolute star, just give your hand again, look at that hand, now sleep and stand, sleep and stand, sleep, sleep, sleep. This time when you wake up you will go and tell everyone you pass that you have just served Denzel Washington. 1, 2 wide awake.

He did. He gratefully took an autograph too.

8.0 Back in the room.

As you have taken someone into hypnosis and they have done your bidding it is only fair that you bring them out. If you do not, they will emerge from hypnosis, eventually, but they might feel a little disorientated. Because they are taking directions you can ensure they come out of hypnosis cleanly and it is a great opportunity to ensure that when they return to normal awareness they will be feeling fantastic and ready to go in every way.

It ensures your back is covered if they immediately go outside and walk under a bus. You could simply clap your hands and say 'Eyes open, wide awake'. But that is not doing the job effectively. A good wake up ratifies the work you have done, gives an opportunity for them to go back into a trance instantly if you wish to give them this ability and ensures they are back to normal in every way.

In a moment I am going to count from one to five and on the count of five your eyes will open and you will be back at full conscious wakeful alertness, everything back to normal in every way. It will be like you have woken up from a wonderful nights sleep. You will understand hypnosis is not sleep but the next time you get in bed and sleep you will sleep wonderfully, better than you have for years and awake at an appropriate time refreshed revitalised, feeling brand new.

One. Feeling less relaxed now, every muscle nerve and fibre coming alive.

Two. A surge of energy is pouring in through your fingers, toes, up arms, legs, spine to the top of your head.

Three. Take a deep breath, fill your chest with energy giving oxygen, it spreads to every muscle nerve and fibre.

Four. Take another as your head is being washed through with cool clear spring water, your entire body washed through, refreshed and revitalised.

Five. Eyes open wide awake/back in the room.

Or alternatively

On the count of five you will be back at normal awareness, everything back to normal, feeling fantastic.

One. Feeling wonderful.
Two. To achieve your goals.
Three. With a feeling of freedom.
Four. Feel the force of that feeling.
Five. Eyes open feeling wonderfully alive.

I will often clap my hands on the count of five to add to the effect. This tends to startle the subject a little and really puts some distance between the state they were in and the wide awake state. In this moment the doors to their hypnotic world close. It encourages amnesia for the experience. You can further encourage this by immediately asking them a question that does not relate to the hypnotic experience they have just had. This could be related to a conversation you were having with them prior to the hypnosis, or just a trivial question. When they then try to recall the hypnotic experience they do so with the same ineffectiveness they might try to recall a dream that seemed vivid just moments earlier.

So how long have you had your motorbike?

Is that your glass on the floor?

Is it a little warm in here?

9.0 Safety Last.

Health and safety is almost completely in control of the hypnotist. Being The Hypnotist brings responsibility with it. Be the best you can be and treat your subjects with the respect they deserve. Always demonstrate that you care and they are in safe and competent hands. This makes the job easier anyway. Always do a proper wake up. Do not take silly risks. Giving someone full body catalepsy and balancing them between chairs is an impressive sight – but the subject may have a back condition. The chairs may collapse. Telling someone they are an Olympic swimmer might encourage them to lay down on a table top and do front crawl or might result in them diving off of a table head first. Do not take unnecessary risks. Shouting 'Sleep' as the subject is running from one end of the room to another could result in them dropping to the floor and smashing a hip. So encourage them to stop running, to stand still, let them know that their legs will support them. Say 'Sleep and stand'. Show your subject twice the amount of respect and attention you would in the normal waking state. Ensure that your suggestion includes remarks that they will not do anything that will hurt them or anyone else.

9.1 Abreactions and other surprises.

Very rarely when a subject is hypnotized they have a large emotional reaction that surprises them and if unprepared The Hypnotist too. So be prepared. They may be upset and cry, often with complete abandon. Equally they may crack up laughing. Sometimes they know why they are upset and sometimes they do not. An abreaction like this is nothing to be afraid of, managed appropriately you are not going to do anyone damage here and can ensure they come through it better off- if a little shaken. It could be something you have said has acted as a trigger that has reminded them of something traumatic or a memory with negative emotions associated with it and they have plunged back into the memory in the first person. Keep your directions clean. Do not regress people to places that could have been hurtful or harmful or frightening. Do not regress to their childhood. The stage hypnotist can safely make people act like a six year old but should not regress someone to their own life at six – just in case it was awful. Sometimes it seems an abreaction is quite spontaneous – without any particular trigger. It is as if emotions we do our up most to ignore and outbursts we need to have but suppress can lurk just beneath the surface of consciousness. Hypnosis is an opportunity for them to get out, often as soon as the conscious mind is out of the way. There is no need to alarm the subject by getting freaked out and upset. If you are not going to start doing impromptu therapy then the best thing is to simply tell them that everything will be OK, that you spend some time with them and that in a moment you will bring them back up and they do not need to bring these memories and feelings back with them. Then do a proper wake up. Spend some time with them afterwards to ensure they are OK. Of course as a hypnotherapist an abreaction is an opportunity to deal with something. You have often found a 'splinter' and can start to pull it out. But this is not a book on therapy. Stick with what you know. Do not suggest they have issues and should seek therapy either. They are likely to know why whatever it is that came up came up and can make their own decisions.

On occasion a subject may get a little concerned as they feel they are going into a trance – if they associate this with losing control. If they have had panic attacks or a bad experience with drugs they may associate it with that. If they still wish to be hypnotized then it is important to let them feel in control and know that they can manage the depth they go to. This can be achieved by training them to take themselves in and out.

Even more rarely someone may have a fit, perhaps they suffer from epilepsy or sleep apnea. If they are not thrashing around when fitting but have instead become very rigid it can be difficult to spot immediately. Although in my opinion there is no more likelihood that someone is going to fit in hypnosis than anywhere else, I am not a medical man. So do not take that advice. Use the precautionary principle. Recognise it can happen. Not all epileptic people know they have the condition.

If someone is in this position then you quickly do what St. John's Ambulance Service tells you to do. Basic Health and Safety training is inexpensive. It will teach you how to save lives and much more in one day. If you are not up for doing this then you should ask people if they have any serious health conditions, and refuse to hypnotize them.

Recognise that if you are going to have your subject doing things that involve moving around that they should be doing this with their eyes open. Just because you have hypnotized the waitress to make you free coffee does not mean she should risk getting scalded. Dancing with the eyes closed can be dangerous too.

If you are going to hypnotize someone and tell them you have stolen their voice/balls/favourite fairy and tell them this will make them angry there is nothing to stop them hitting you. Unless of course you tell them that they will get angry but will not actually get violent. If you are going to suggest a disgusting taste into your subject's mouth then tell them they may feel sick but that they won't actually be sick.

Getting people to eat and drink things when hypnotized is also asking for trouble. Although in the vast majority of cases it will be fine – you never know if they have an allergy to something.

Using catalepsy with people who have arthritic conditions is obviously not advised.

I could go on. Think. Use common sense and a bit more. Look at the surrounding environment. Remove or steer clear of potential dangers. Be safe. Show you care.

9.2 Morals and Ethics

It is often stated by hypnotists that you cannot make people do things they would not normally do and certainly cannot make people do things that go against their morals and ethics. I absolutely disagree. Please keep in mind that morals and ethics are just a surface veneer maintained for social acceptance. When the conscious critical mind is out of the equation it is possible and likely that moral and ethical boundaries are too. So in this sense you are responsible for the moral and ethical boundaries. The subject remains human and is capable of a full range of responses. Again I suggest you use common sense. Understand that the routines I have outlined in this book are there for entertainment purposes. I am in no way suggesting that you commit crimes or abuse the knowledge given.

When hypnotising you are not making people do things against their will you are instead bending their reality so that the subjects will has an interest in following your direction. I repeat you are responsible for the moral and ethical boundaries.

9.3 Final thoughts

Throughout any of my training courses I emphasise that it is important to look beyond technique and let what you do become your art form. Practise, observe, stretch yourself – there is always more to learn. Then relax and do your work. There is no need to settle for being an average hypnotist – be the best you can be.

Of course at first it is important to get your technique mastered so work hard to do this. Once it is, be prepared to let your intuition guide you about how you apply this knowledge. Human beings are suggestible. Take that understanding and knowledge with you into every walk of life whether you are speaking to your children, at work or presenting an idea.

The words are not as important as the ideas. The techniques are not as important as your intention. You can these words and techniques if you want, but make them better still. If you like them take these ideas and make them your own. Observe your subject; they will give you all the guidance you need.

Aim to leave your subjects and your audience with a new view of the world, give them an experience they will still recount 20 years from now.

10.0 References

(1) Bernheim, H. (Herter, C.A. trans.), **De la Suggestion et de son Application à la Thérapeutique, [Second Edition], 1887.** (Suggestive Therapeutics: A Treatise on the Nature and Uses of Hypnotism,) G.P. Putnam's Sons, (New York), 1889.

(2) Pattie, Frank A. **Mesmer and Animal Magnetism: A Chapter in the History of Medicine.** Edmonston Publishing, Inc, 1994.

(3) Braid, James. **Magic, witchcraft, animal magnetism, hypnotism and electro-biology.** London. 3rd edition 1852.

(4) Erickson, Milton H. **Life Reframing in Hypnosis**. Ernest L. Rossi (Editor), Margaret O. Ryan (Editor). 1985

(5) Elman, Dave. **Hypnotherapy – Findings in Hypnosis.** 1964

(6) Griffin, Joe and Tyrell, Ivan. **Human Givens – A New Approach to Emotional Health and Clear Thinking**. HG Publishing. 2003.

(7) Southon, Mike and West, Chris. **The Beermat Entrepreneur – Turning your good idea into a great business.** Prentice Hall. 2002.

(8) Charcot, J.M. **Physiologie pathologique. Sur les divers états nerveux déterminés par l'hypnotisation chez les hystériques.** [Pathological physiology: On the various nervous states determined by the hypnotisation of hystericals]. Comptes rendus de l'Académie Des Sciences, **94, 403-405. 1882.**

(9) Overdurf, John and Silverthorn, Julie. **Training Trances.** Metamorphous Press, 1994.

(10) Rossi, Ernest L. and Cheek David B. **Mind Body Therapy – Methods of Ideodynamic Healing in Hypnosis.** WW. Norton. 1988.

(11) McGill, Ormond. **The New Encyclopedia of Stage Hypnotism.** CHP. 1996.

(12) Overdurf, John and Silverthorn, Julie. **Training Trances.** Metamorphous Press, 1994.

(13) Jermay, Luke. **Building Blocks**. Alakazam Magic. 2003.

(14) Grinder, John and Bandler, Richard. **Trance-Formations: Neuro-Linguistic Programming and the Structure of Hypnosis.** Moab, UT: Real People Press. 1981.

(15) Chase, Jon. **Deeper and Deeper – Secrets of Stage Hypnosis.** AHA Ltd.. 2005

(16) Rossi, Ernest. **The Psychobiology of Mind Body Healing**, W.W.Norton. 1986

(18) Chase, Jon. **Deeper and Deeper – Secrets of Stage Hypnosis.** AHA Ltd.. 2005